Praise for Dubravka Ugresic

"On the grim state of the book business, several writings have been published lately—some excellent—by editors and publishers who have seen things go from bad to worse, and who now help explain why this has happened. Dubravka Ugresic adds immeasurably to that still-modest bibliography. *Thank You for Not Reading* is an indispensable critique as well as an exhilarating work of prose—a brilliant meditation on the literary, cultural, and existential consequences of the global triumph of the Bottom Line. For this dazzling collection only starts with Ugresic's sharp (and frequently hilarious) analysis of publishing, soon moving on to the far larger, deeper problem of what life is like throughout the world today. This book is something rare indeed: a work as pleasurable to read as it is edifying; as marvelously crafted, line by line, as it is wise throughout."—Mark Crispin Miller

"A brilliant, enthralling spread of storytelling and high-velocity reflections. . . . Ugresic is a writer to follow. A writer to be cherished."—Susan Sontag

"Ugresic must be numbered among what Jacques Maritain called the dreamers of the true; she draws us into the dream."—Richard Eder, *New York Times*

"Like Nabokov, Ugresic affirms our ability to remember as a source for saving our moral and compassionate identity."—John Balaban, *Washington Post*

"Dubravka Ugresic is the philosopher of evil and exile, and the storyteller of many shattered lives the wars in the former Yugoslavia produced. . . . Utterly original, beautiful, and supremely intelligent."—Charles Simic

Thank You for Not Reading

Essays on Literary Trivia

Dubravka Ugresic

Translated from the Croatian by Celia Hawkesworth
with the assistance of Damion Searles

DALKEY ARCHIVE PRESS

Originally published in Dutch as *Verboden te lezen!* (Breda, 2001)

The epigraphs at the beginning of the seven sections belong to Eeyore, the unforgettable character from *The World of Pooh* by A. A. Milne.

Library of Congress Cataloging-in-Publication Data

Ugrešić, Dubravka.
   [Zabranjeno citanje. English]
   Thank you for not reading : essays on literary trivia / Dubravka Ugrešić ; translated from the Croatian by Celia Hawkesworth.
     p. cm.
   ISBN 1-56478-298-0 (alk. paper)
   1. Publishers and publishing. 2. Authorship. 3. Books and reading. I. Hawkesworth, Celia, 1942– II. Title.

Z278.U3613 2003
070.5—dc22

                               2003055099

Partially funded by a grant from the Illinois Arts Council, a state agency.

Dalkey Archive Press books are published by the Center for Book Culture, a nonprofit organization.

www.centerforbookculture.org

Printed on permanent/durable acid-free paper and bound in the United States of America.

Contents

1. Opening

2. Good Morning

3. The Market

4. Country Cousin

5. Life without a Tail

6. Well, Goodbye

7. Closing

Acknowledgments

Thank You for Not Reading is the result of the inner struggle between two of the author's creative impulses. One whispered in the author's ear that self-respecting writers should not write about things that wise people prefer not to discuss. The second impulse dragged the author in the opposite direction: self-respecting writers should never try to be too wise. This feud was the source of many features of the book: its title, style, tone, and rhythm.

This is why *Thank You for Not Reading* is half fiction and half fact, or maybe a little more than half fiction. I wrote some of the essays under the mask of an East European grumbler confused by the dynamics of the global book market, hence all the quotes from Eeyore, the best-known grumbler in literary history. Although I usually tried to avoid it, sometimes the tone of the "professor of literature" managed to sneak into the essays. In other essays, the reader may feel the struggle between two intentions: the author's ambition to take the things seriously and the fear that if she does, she'll bore her readers. However, every time this light book was on the verge of becoming as serious as its theme deserves, the memory of a student of mine returned to warn me. When asked what makes a good book good, he answered without hesitation: "It has to sparkle!" I can't say whether this one sparkles, but I certainly tried to meet my student's literary standards.

This book is not objective and does not try to be. Some readers may find my unwillingness to use scholarly conventions (such as footnotes or proper bibliographical data) impolite. I have been reading, or at least leafing through, some of the scholarly and less scholarly books that deal with a similar theme. Some were written long ago, some during the time I was writing my book, and some, such as *The Business of Books* by André Schiffrin and *Book Business* by Jason Epstein, appeared in the bookstores at the same time as the first publication of my book, in Dutch. All in all, *Thank You for Not Reading* corresponds in one way or another with a list of authors, ideas, tendencies, magazines such as the *Baffler,* and books such as *Conglomerates and the Media* (ed. Erik Barnouw); *The Gutenberg Elegies* by Sven Birkerts; *Amusing Ourselves to Death* by Neil Postman; *On Television* and other books by Pierre Bourdieu; *The Death of Literature* by Alvin Kernan; *Talents and Technicians* by John W. Aldridge; *Does Literary Studies Have a Future?* by Eugene Goodheart; *Bad* by Paul Fussell; *Carnival Culture* by James B. Twitchell; *Kitsch and Art* by Tomas Kulka; *Modernity at Large* by Arjun Appadurai; *Understanding Popular Culture* by John Fiske; *The Future of the Book* (ed. Geoffrey Nunberg); *The Wake of Art* and *After the End of Art* by Arthur C. Danto; *Fahrenheit 451* by Ray Bradbury; *Six Memos for the Next Millennium* and *The Uses of Literature* by Italo Calvino; *Life: The Movie* by Neal Gabler; *A History of Reading* by Alberto Manguel; *One Market under God* by Thomas Frank; *Cynicism and Postmodernity* by Timothy Bewes; *The Cultures of Globalization* (ed. Fredric Jameson and Masao Miyoshi); *Globalization* by Zygmunt Bauman; *Representations of the Intellectual* by Edward W. Said; *On Grief and Reason* by Joseph Brodsky; *Altogether Elsewhere: Writers On Exile* (ed. Marc Robinson).

Every time I visited the United States as a visiting lecturer, I realized once again that besides the loud and visible literary life and its trivia—the theme of my book—there is a less visible and quiet one, in the university. Spring semester of 2002 I taught in the Department of Slavic Languages and Literatures at Harvard University. My students Jacob Emery, Rebecca Reich, Marijeta Bozovic, Dehn Gilmore, Katharine Holt, Anna Gessen, David

Elmer, and Steven Segal were all superior readers and interpreters of literary texts. I am sorry that my book was already finished: it could have been spared some of its darker tones and disbelief in the future of literature. Literature does have a future: my students.

I would like to thank my agent Laura Susijn and my publisher, Dalkey Archive Press, surely the most appropriate home for this book. I would also like to thank my editor Chad W. Post, for the fastest and easiest publishing offer in my literary career. At the time the offer reached me, Damion Searls, a Fulbright fellow in Amsterdam, generously offered to read the manuscript. I am very grateful for his wise interventions, both stylistic and substantive.

For their encouragement on this and other occasions, I'd like to thank Meredith Tax, Svetlana Boym, Ellen Ellias, Beka Vuco, Madeline Levin, Ivana Vuletic, Michael Flier, Charles Simic, Larry Wolf, Erica Goldman, Priscilla Meyer, Ellen Hendler-Spitz, Cynthia Simmons, Martha Saxton, Liz Arney, Susan Sontag, Florence Ladd, and Michael Henry Heim.

First and last, I warmly thank my translator Celia Hawkesworth for the long friendship and effort she put into the translation of this and my other books.

I sit at my desk.
My life is grotesque.
         —Joseph Brodsky

1 ─────── Opening

"Hallo, Eeyore," they called out cheerfully.
"Ah!" said Eeyore, "Lost your way?"

Los Torcedores

About ten years ago, I was at the opening of the annual London Book Fair. The fair was opened formally by Joan Collins. Her first novel had just come out and the famous American-British actress, newly baptized writer, and full sister of Jackie Collins, was a perfectly credible person to open a book fair. Joan Collins appeared, dressed like a quotation: in a little pink Chanel suit, with a pink pillbox hat on her head and a coquettish veil over her eyes. Hypnotized, I was swept along in the crowd of visitors, which was swept along after the television cameras, which were swept along after Joan. With puckered lips, Joan fingered the books on display, as though she were fingering Victoria's Secret lingerie.

What does this all have to do with literature? Almost nothing. Then why mention something as trivial as Joan Collins's pink suit? Because trivia has swamped contemporary literary life and become, it seems, more important than the books. A book's blurb is more important than the book itself, the author's photograph on the book jacket is more important than its content, the author's appearance in wide-circulation newspapers and on TV is more important than what that author has actually written.

Many writers feel increasingly uncomfortable in such a literary landscape, densely populated with publishers, editors, agents, distributors, brokers, publicity specialists, bookstore chains, "marketing people," television cameras, photographers. The writer and his reader—the two most important links in the chain—are more isolated than ever.

So what is left for the writer? Pretend not to notice and fatalistically accept eternity as a measure of value? Eternity, indeed! When the lifespan of a book is some thirty years in peacetime (less in war), before paper bacteria turns it into mush. Take his bearings from some higher literary justice? Justice, indeed! When bad books are ever more frequently inflated, and good ones ignored. Count on the reader? The reader, indeed! When the reader is beguiled by what is in front of his nose: powerful bookstore chains, airport shops and Amazon.com.

The writer who does not accept the rules of the market will simply perish. The reader who does not accept what the market offers him is condemned to literary fasting or rereading the books he has already read. The writer and his reader—those for whom literature exists—today live a semi-underground life. The world of the literary market is ruled by the producers of books, but producing books does not quite mean producing literature.

As a reader, I long for my own writer. I sift through books with promising blurbs, but few of them satisfy my readerly tastes. Bookstores increasingly resemble gleaming supermarkets: the products look high-quality, but the flavor is disappointing. Just as fruit and vegetables have mutated and lost their flavor in favor of external appearance, so books too, both bad and good, have mutated with time into mainstream literature.

As a writer, I long for my own reader.

A year or two ago, a letter arrived for me from Guatemala:

I spent the weekend in Guatemala City, and stayed at the Princess Hotel. I prefer that hotel to the Plaza las Americas, where the nouveaux riches of Guatemala gather. The Princess cultivates a British style: subdued lights, walls with dark wood paneling, everything somehow velvety and soft. I was sitting there, in the lobby. At the next table were two young Americans. They looked like businessmen, in white dress shirts and ties, but, as Americans often do, they were talking too loudly. So instead of reading my newspaper, I was obliged to listen to their conversation. Suddenly, to my great surprise, I realized that they were not talking about commercial strategies for securing the Guatemala market, but about literature. And what can I tell you, you won't believe me in any case, they mentioned your name, almost lovingly. It crossed my mind to go over to them and say that I was a friend of yours, but I didn't, you know how shy I am. That little episode kept me in a good mood the whole day.

That was what my friend who had ended up in Guatemala wrote. Of course I didn't believe him, but his letter put me in a good mood too, for several days. I imagined the wonderful Guatemalan landscapes (although I've never been there) as a background against which two of *my* devoted readers in white shirts were holding an *almost loving* (that especially appealed to me) conversation about *my* book.

Incidentally, since we are on that side of the world, I learned recently that Cuban cigar-makers, *los torcedores,* are the most educated segment of Cuba's population. Rolling cigars by hand is, evidently, tedious and laborious work. The cigar-makers sit on benches, as in school, and spend the whole day rolling leaves of tobacco in their hands. But there is a tradition in Cuba of hiring readers, who sit on a raised platform, hold a book and a microphone in their hands, and read. The cigar-makers roll the tobacco leaves in their hands and listen.

I imagine a stuffy workshop, heavy tropical heat, buzzing flies, the sweaty brows of the cigar-makers who sleepily roll the tobacco leaves and drink in the words gurgling out of the microphone. In my fantasy there is no room for Castro's speeches. The Cuban cigar-makers listen to the works of literature. Each cigar is soaked with human sweat, with the rhythm of the words pouring out of the microphone and those which hum like an echo in the listeners' sleepy heads.

The listeners in my Cuban fantasy are not passive. On the contrary, in the many years of their working lives they have listened to the most select pages of world literature, their literary taste is as sharp as a razor, they react to every badly used word, to every false note. And if they don't like what they are hearing, they express their dissatisfaction loudly and pelt the poor reader with heavy cigars.

They say that the best Cuban cigar costs around four hundred dollars. If it were up to me, I would make them cost three times more. For if the worthy Cuban *torcedores* have listened to a whole library during their working lives, then the cigar might as well have been made by George Steiner himself.

As far as George Steiner is concerned, I doubt whether university professors can afford a Cuban cigar. But Joan Collins can. She is a best-selling writer, so let her pay for a cigar! I imagine the circle closing like that. I am also consoled by the thought that literary justice, however feeble, nevertheless circulates somehow, no matter how narrow and roundabout its paths.

As far as I am concerned, I have decided to take matters into my own hands and help literary justice a bit. I admit that I sometimes go in for a little fabrication, but what can I do, fabrication is my trade. So, for instance, I recently sent a letter to a friend of mine, an excellent writer:

Dear M. W.,

A month ago I spent a few days in Memphis. I visited the famous Arcade Restaurant on 540 South Street, and ordered the obvious: a hamburger and a Coke. The waiter was a young boy, an Indian of rather listless appearance. Since my order was taking forever to arrive, I went to the counter to find him. I know that you won't believe me, but there, hidden behind the counter, I found the boy sitting on an overturned plastic bin completely absorbed in your book. . . .

2000

2 ──────── Good Morning

Piglet explained to Tigger that he mustn't mind what Eeyore said because he was *always* gloomy; and Eeyore explained to Piglet that, on the contrary, he was feeling particularly cheerful this morning.

Literary Dreams

In a market-oriented literary culture, things are hardest for the proletariat, for us writers. Of all my fellow writers, I feel the sorriest for the East Europeans, perhaps because I myself belong to that disreputable crew.

For years, American and West European writers mocked their East European colleagues because of their sinecures: their free dental care, free apartments, free writers' union holiday homes *(dom tvorchestva)* and more rarely a free country cottage *(dacha)*. But they cunningly kept quiet about their own sinecures: their creative-writing posts, scholarships, funding and foundations, projects, state-subsidized books and translations into foreign languages, and free artists' holiday homes *(writers' retreats)*. Today, the Western writers still have theirs, while the Easterners have found themselves with nothing.

I must admit that this *nothing* makes me dizzy. Every night I have nightmares, I feel very *Slavic,* as someone on the sitcom *Ellen* once put it ("I feel so moody, so dark, so depressed, almost Slavic!").

For instance, I dreamed about a large outdoor market. We are all there, a great crowd of farmers, everyone selling what he himself has grown. On the counter in front of me are three humble beets. The great Russian writer Nikolai Vasilevich Gogol stops at the counter. "Your beets have grown well in your garden," he says. "They look more like potatoes than beets."

I dreamed that my teeth were falling out one by one and turning into the volumes of my future collected works. And the volumes were called *Incisor, Molar, Canine, . . .*

I dreamed that I was a member of a small tribe which lives in Siberian forests, and that I was creating a national literature from the beginnings of their literacy until today. And I was inscribing those beginnings in the tanned hide of a Siberian reindeer.

I dreamed that I was Jorge Luis Borges, miraculously resurrected and able to see, and he tapped his hand on his brow and turned into Paul Coelho.

On the whole I dream terrible dreams. Not long ago I dreamed that I had been captured by Radovan Karadžić, the war criminal, who tortured me by reciting his poems for children and adults. He even made me learn the poems by heart, and he tested me every day.

I also dreamed that I was the greatest writer of a small country in the south of Europe, called Croatia, and that the president of the country gave me a medal.

"Congratulations, Mr. Finkielkraut!" said the president, as he hanged the medal round my neck and then, in the manner of communist leaders, gives me a smacking kiss on the lips.

"But I'm not Finkielkraut!" I shouted, utterly appalled. No one noticed, they all applauded enthusiastically.

I also dreamed that I was Joan Collins, that I had been awarded the Nobel Prize for Literature, and that I was writing my acceptance speech for Stockholm. In my dream, I sweated and shook with fear, although I didn't know what made me so afraid: receiving the Nobel Prize or receiving it as Joan Collins. Not even the fact that I was more than sixty years old and looked thirty was any comfort.

In the same genre, I dreamed that I was Ivana Trump and that I had been elected president of the International PEN club. That dream was far more agreeable, because after my election as president, we all went off to the Plaza, where my fellow writers could order afternoon tea at $18.99 each.

I dreamed that Fyodor Mikhailovich Dostoyevsky kept phoning me from his grave.

"*Ah, koleshka, ty moja koleshka . . .*" he sighs.

"I'm not a colleague of yours! Why don't you leave me alone!" I shout.

Deathly silence from the receiver.

In my last dream I was Salman Rushdie and I gave all the money I had earned to a fund for the protection of Algerian writers and other writers under threat. For some reason that dream upset me so much that I went to my therapist.

"Why don't you simply change your job?"

"What do you mean *simply?* Stop being a writer?"

"Why not! Reinvent yourself," advised the helpful therapist.

I followed his advice. I got a job as a waitress in a Portuguese restaurant. One of my co-workers sometimes recites Pessoa to me after work, over a glass of wine, but that is pretty much my only contact with literature. I no longer have literary nightmares. I dream pleasant, refreshing dreams. For example, I dream that I am a waitress in a Portuguese restaurant who serves her guests while flying; I am Superwaitress. As they leave, my clients throw me a tip, which I modestly catch in flight, accompanied by the enthusiastic applause of those present.

1996

Book Proposal

Writing a book proposal is one of the most important skills in a market-oriented literary culture. The book proposal is the cornerstone, without which there is no book. That is why the handbook *How to Write a Successful Book Proposal* ought to be the Bible of every author who wants to be "a confident player in today's fiercely competitive book publishing industry."

"Okay, okay . . ." mumbles the editor into the telephone receiver. "I've received your manuscript, but I've no intention of doing anything until you send a book proposal."

What is a book proposal? A summary of the book, a short synopsis. What is a successful book proposal? One that gets the editor to read the manuscript. What is a really successful book proposal? One that gets the editor to buy the book before it has even been written.

A successful book proposal must have a hook, or bait, or glue. At least that's what the author of the above-mentioned manual suggests. It must hold the editor's attention and delay, if not prevent, the proposal's flight into the trashcan.

"I just can't find the hook," complains Ellen. My fellow writer has quite given up working on her book and has spent months writing the perfect proposal. "I'd rather write a novel than two pages of synopsis," she says.

"Imagine you are writing a personal ad, maybe it'll go better," I foolishly try to console her.

A successful book proposal must also answer the question of what type of readership the book is intended for. I can sort of understand the hook business, but I just can't imagine my readership in advance.

"Imagine that you are writing for Harrison Ford, maybe it'll go better," suggests Ellen.

Ellen does not realize how right she is. For a book proposal is nothing other than a screenplay, an effective account of an imagined film.

The nineteenth century, France, a young woman married to a provincial doctor dreams of love. Torn between a tedious husband and one lover, then another, burdened with debts accumulating daily, the woman commits suicide. The book is intended for a wide female readership.

"Good," says the editor. "Just change the nineteenth century to the twentieth, and add another lover or two. Give the husband a bit of fun as well, let him turn out to be gay. And forget the suicide at the end! No one would believe that."

The nineteenth century, Russia, a married woman belonging to high society falls in love, leaves her husband and son, lives as a social outcast with her adored lover, and when he leaves her to go to war, she throws herself under a train. The book is intended for a wide female readership.

"Great!" says the editor. "Two sisters, one lives in Soviet Russia married to an KGB officer, she falls in love with a dissident. The other emigrates and marries a boring, provincial French doctor. In 1990, the sisters meet. Flashbacks, two different lives, two female destinies. The illusions and disillusions of East and West after the fall of communism. Title: *Two Sisters*. Start writing!"

My first success encouraged me. I even became obsessive. Recently I have done nothing but write book proposals. I took the trouble to write a book proposal for *Remembrance of Things Past*. It was turned down. Boring, too long, change the title. . . .

Now I'm testing the market. Camouflaged Shakespeare works great. *Ulysses* got nowhere. Despite my having told it as a soap opera, *The Man Without Qualities* ended up in the trash. *Memoirs of Hadrian* too, and *The Death of Virgil*. All right, I agree, the great European writers were always a bit tedious. But even Hemingway didn't do any better, although I did manage to sell *The Old Man and the Sea*. I disguised it a bit. I stressed the ecological aspect of the whole thing. And I changed the old man into a good-looking young Cuban exile, gay. The proposal was immediately accepted.

All in all, I think that I have learned something. Why do people like gossip? Because people are always interested in what happens to other people. Gossip is the last remaining form of concern for other people. In literature gossip is the most basic literary genre. A successful book proposal is successful gossip. Best-sellers are nothing but extended gossip. Many great literary works are great tracts of gossip. *War and Peace,* for example. Tolstoy was a master, he knew his craft. The Bible, the cornerstone of Western literature, is the greatest, the most exciting and, incidentally, the most profitable book of gossip of all time. Greek mythology is nothing but grandiose family gossip. Enduringly exciting mythologies are gossip about gods.

I'm not complaining. Except that I haven't written a line for ages. I mean, a literary line of my own. I'm completely absorbed in these book proposals. I'm becoming increasingly impudent. I camouflage less and less. I've just sent an editor a proposal for *One Hundred Years of Solitude*.

"Forget the contents!" said the editor. "No one could possibly follow that story. But there's no reason not to use that great title."

1996

Agents and Scouts

A couple years ago, I spent a year as a lecturer in literature at a small American university. From previous visits, I had learned several routine bureaucratic things that a foreigner has to do upon arrival. One was getting health insurance. In the office for foreign lecturers and students I was offered a form which I filled in neatly and attached a check to. All that remained were some details that had to be explained by my insurance agent. I called the insurance office. They gave me the name of my agent, Skip Woody, but he was not available at the moment. I left my phone number. Skip Woody did not call. After three months of calling in vain, I decided to look for Skip Woody in person. Skip Woody was not available, again, but in the office they advised me to change the shabby health insurance, for which Skip Woody was responsible, to something better. I completed a new form and attached a check. This time the agent I was supposed to contact about the details did not have a name, but a number: 3424. After some time, I called the office and asked to speak to agent 3424. 3424 was not available either. Another month went by and I called again.

"I need to speak to agent 3424," I said to the secretary after a long wait.

"Oh, Skip Woody! I'm afraid he's not available at the moment."

This phantom health insurance agent, Skip Woody, remained unknown to me in both insurance companies until the end of my stay. I paid my modest medical bills out of my own pocket. The fact that I had not one but two health insurance policies did not help.

"You had bad luck," said the colleague to whom I complained, shrugging her shoulders, as though it were a matter of a lottery and not a paid service.

It is similar with literary agents: I have bad luck with them as well. They are never available. I think it is easier to get the White House on the phone than the living voice of a literary agent. One's contact with a literary agent always remains obscure.

All of my literary agents have been women. Three had secretaries: young, attractive, kindly, well-read men. I had only seen male secretaries in soap operas: first in *Dynasty,* where the wicked Alexis exploited the services of the good-looking Dexter, and then in *The Bold and the Beautiful,* where older working women were surrounded by attractive young men who served them with ardor.

Where are literary agents recruited? I wouldn't know, but the agents I knew graduated from neither Princeton nor Yale. The first was a housewife bored with her marital routine, so she decided to embark on a business venture which cost nothing (she charged me for postal costs and took ten percent of my fee) and brought contacts which dispelled her provincial boredom. The other had been a bank clerk before becoming an agent (she took fifteen percent of my fee).

The third had been the secretary at a literary agency before becoming its owner. She agreed to put me on her list, because of a recommendation from an established writer. That was the end of it. I did try to call her, but she always forgot my name and who I was, every time.

"I'm the one you have charged a percentage to four times already!" I said.

"Hmm . . ." she mumbled indifferently. "What did you say your name was?"

Later I learned why she couldn't remember my name: she had over three hundred authors on her list.

The fourth did remember my name, but could not remember the names of publishers. She confused Feltrinelli and fettucine, Gallimard and Gauloises, Einaudi and Audi. She took her fifteen percent for work she did not do, unless sending a contract for a signature counts as work.

Agents, scouts, and subagents have woven their webs over the entire contemporary literary market, like spiders. Scouts sniff around, mingle, and party, proving that even a lifestyle can be a profession. They listen to gossip about recent literary production and incidentally remember the names of new writers. They pass the names on to agents and subagents. Subagents and agents are closely connected, just like Skip Woody and agent number 3424. An English agent, for example, will have a French subagent, who in turn has an English subagent—the same person. If a writer leaves one agent and moves to another, the second may be just the subagent of the first. After such experiences, the writer has no choice but to abandon himself to uneasy paranoia and go helplessly round and round in the same circle. How things look at the very peak of the literary jet set, where famous agents surf, I don't know, but I imagine it's similar. Except that far, far more money is involved.

As far as paranoia and social games are concerned, it seems that a large number of agents, just like a large number of writers in the literary marketplace, is a necessary evil. In the world of the jet set, wealthy party-givers, socialites, star-editors, star-agents, star-publishers; in the world of the media conglomerates, where publishing itself is only an incidental business which doesn't make much money; in the world where the one-time fee of a catering-artist (a cook) exceeds the advance of a serious writer several times over; in the world of TV stars; in the world where the memoirs of Monica Lewinsky get a thousand times more publicity than the collected works of Marcel Proust; in the world of the powerful, in other words, things happen differently. Exactly how, I wouldn't know, I haven't been there.

And so, I think of my first agent with a certain tenderness. Several years ago, at a European book fair, the loudspeaker suddenly announced my name. The summons for me to meet someone at the meeting point was even repeated three times. When I made it to the meeting point, my agent was waiting for me.

"Wasn't that a good idea!" she said cheerfully.

"What?"

"Your name was repeated over the loudspeaker three times!"

My agent did not charge me anything for her fresh new idea for promoting her author. Use of the loudspeaker was free.

And I continue my search for an agent, hoping always that one day I will find the right one. Some time ago, I found an agent with a Ph.D. in Classics from Yale. Encouraged by his references, I sent him my manuscript. After a while, a letter arrived:

I have read your manuscript. It is an elegant, unusual, and unconventional work. In other words, it would be hard to find American publishers who would buy such an essentially "European" work. As a lover of European literature, it is hard for me to acknowledge that the battle against the resistance of American publishers (and readers) to European prose is in vain. There are exceptions, of course, but they are rare. I would like to be of more help and to be able to respond more optimistically.

With great respect, cordially yours,

At the same time, a letter arrived from a French agent:

I have not read your manuscript, but I do not doubt that it is an exceptional literary work. However, it would be hard to sell it at this time to any West European publisher. East Europeans are no longer the trend, which is of course sad, but true. If Solzhenitsyn has problems finding a publisher, then there is nothing we can do but wait for happier times.

With warm greetings,

At the same time, a letter arrived from my former Croatian publisher:

Hey, you've been on the blacklist for ten years, it's natural that your readers have forgotten you! Not more than a dozen people would buy one of your books today. No one reads local writers anymore. They hate anti-regime writers, while regime writers make them sick. Books are expensive. It comes to the same thing, one way or another. Only the Croatian edition of Mein Kampf *has sold really well. So there you are.*

Yours,

1999

Low-Income Writer

A writer who thinks about his literary environment, not just about the writing itself, had best keep quiet. Hold his tongue. Otherwise such a writer cuts away the branch he's sitting on. Birds sitting on a branch would never do that. Poets are a kind of bird, aren't they, they also sing. That's why every writer should remember that there is a poet crouching somewhere inside him.

Since we are on publishing industry terrain, here is an example closer to home. A writer of this sort resembles a worker who, instead of standing meekly at his workplace on the conveyer belt, starts asking how the conveyer belt works, how the factory is structured, what exactly happens to the little nails he is moving from one hand to another. As though he were preparing to become a manager. Such a worker should be fired at once.

Many writers have a problem accepting their own calling. I have myself been known to put "typist" under "Profession" when filling in forms. Now that that nice profession is disappearing, I put "translator." It sounds more serious. Because "translator" is a profession, but "writer" is the devil knows what. Writers have the same problem as alcoholics: they can't confess. Before a conversation with an editor, a literary evening, an interview, any situation in which I have to perform my profession, I take a moment to remind myself: "I am a writer! I am a writer! I am a writer!" I always whisper this to myself in English, probably because the movies I've seen about people in rehab were always American, so that "I am an alcoholic" has stuck in my memory in English.

While one person's self-esteem wanes, another's grows. That is, presumably, how the commercial world is arranged. I say "presumably" because I don't know much about it. But I do know something about my own kind, about writers. If a writer isn't sure that he or she is a writer (and real writers never are), then the sense of his or her own profession isn't real either. So how can such writers charge money for their literary efforts? With difficulty. So the publishing industry profits from the low self-confidence of its producers.

"What do you do for a living?"

"I'm a writer."

"I don't mean that... we're all writers in some way! I'm asking what you do, how you pay the bills?"

A real writer always has problems with low self-confidence, is always consumed by doubt, even when he or she is publicly acknowledged. By winning the Nobel Prize, for instance. Especially then. I once met just such a Nobel laureate, so I know what I'm talking about. Someone with low self-esteem is like a punching bag that anyone can use; whoever passes by gives it a punch. A real writer feels guilty and thinks that what he's doing is unimportant, or useless, or privileged (although he's not paid for it), while other serious people work. Such writers are always in awe of physicists, carpenters and surgeons, and can always be crushed with the greatest of ease, like a worm or a fly.

As soon as he is appealed to in the name of humanism, a writer with low self-esteem immediately foregoes his fee. If people in some country complain about the neglected state of literature, he will agree without a murmur to be published for free. Such a person generally treats money as a gift. He lives from his writing, but not from his earnings. That's why writers with low self-esteem are frequently found in writers' retreats. There, pampered by solitude, a pittance of a scholarship and a little free room, the writer with low self-esteem writes his "masterpiece." When he finishes it, he receives a fee which never exceeds his editor's monthly salary.

The field of literature abounds in humble workers who know their place in the world and who are reconciled to their anonymity. I once met an

American writer whose work I was already familiar with. Her book had been translated and published in the former Yugoslavia with a glamorous cover. The dust jacket boasted a portrait of the shining-eyed author and the note that her book was a best-seller in America. When I went to New York for the first time, an acquaintance of mine, an editor in the publishing house that had published the book, asked me to visit the writer. I had never met a living American writer before, let alone a best-selling one. The address sounded intoxicating: Brooklyn Heights. When I rang the bell, the door was opened by a plump middle-aged woman, the writer's secretary, I thought. But she was the author herself. By the time I arrived in New York, the photograph from the dust jacket was no longer compatible with the live model. It turned out that Serbo-Croatian was the only language her book had been translated into.

"Say hello to my readers in Yugoslavia," she said, with charming melancholy.

She lived in a little basement apartment, with mattresses scattered in the hall. It later emerged that the writer gave lessons in belly dancing, hence the mattresses.

"That's what I live on," she said.

The writer took me on a little walk around Brooklyn Heights.

"This is where Norman Mailer lives," she said, proudly pointing to one house. "I run into him a lot. He sometimes even says hello to me. 'Hello, Mary,' he says...."

My heart still aches when I remember Mary, the melancholy belly dancer and writer. And my writer's fist rises in a sign of protest, but in an indeterminate direction. Did Goethe have to give lessons in belly dancing? I ask. Did Turgenev or Tolstoy? I ask and wait for an answer, but there isn't any.

I know, it would be better for me to hold my tongue. Sing like a bird on a branch, to stick to the feathery metaphor from before. And let's hope someone remembers to scatter a few crumbs.

1996

Long Live Socialist Realism!

I don't know why, but the rules of market-oriented literary culture remind me of good old socialist realism. I admit that my head's a bit muddled from the trauma known as Eastern Europe, but that's what I think. I also admit that I travel too much—here, there, back again—so I see things all mixed up. And maybe it's just nostalgia. But isn't that understandable? My entire country has been destroyed by murderers and criminals, my libraries have been burned by thugs, surely I have a right to nostalgia, at least.

Today there is hardly anyone who knows what socialist realism is. East European artists have an allergic reaction to it. For the last fifty years, East European artists have developed elaborate strategies of subversion and given socialist realism such a hammering that they have killed it stone dead. They were so bloodthirsty that they erased all trace of it. That's why no one can explain what the socialist realist scourge was anymore. For Westerners, and more surprisingly also for Easterners, the idea of socialist realism has been sealed in its monumental icon: Mukhina's *The Worker and Collective Farm Girl (Rabochy i kolhoznitsa)* monument, which also appears as the logo for movies produced by Mosfilm. And, of course, in the figure of the hypothetical father of the term itself, Joseph Stalin.

A brief recap. Socialist realism demands from the artist the truthful, historically concrete depiction of reality in its revolutionary development. This truthfulness and historical concreteness of the artistic depiction of reality must be combined with the task of ideologically remolding and educating the working people in the spirit of socialism. Socialist realist literature must be accessible to the broad mass of readers. This fundamental didactic demand produces a novel structured around the struggle of positive and negative heroes (Superman vs. Lex Luthor!), and various types of novels: the "production novel," the "pedagogical novel," and so on.

If we ignore its victims for a moment, then we can say that the art of socialist realism was a happy art, even when it dealt with darker themes. My personal favorite is the "disability" theme, introduced by Nikolai Ostrovsky in his novel *How the Steel Was Tempered,* which is considered to be an official cornerstone of socialist realist literature. Ostrovsky's novel is a story about a war invalid, a blind man, a positive hero who in the end overcomes everything. The Yugoslav film *Just People* also used this theme. The main characters are a man and a woman: an engineer with a missing leg (a former partisan, a war invalid) and a young, blind doctor. They fall in love. They spend days working hard, he to build the society of the future, she in her hospital. They often go skiing together: the engineer skis on one leg, the doctor by memory. The doctor subjects herself to a risky operation, after which her sight is restored. I shall never erase from my heart the magnificent happy ending, when the limping engineer and the formerly blind woman meet on a mighty socialist dam. Their kiss, accompanied by the mighty roar of the water and the ecstatic applause of the workers, will remain in my cultural memory forever.

The art of socialist realism was not only happy, but also sexy. Nowhere have so many muscular and healthy bodies been put on display, so many entwined haymakers and tractor drivers, workers and peasants, strong men and women. Nowhere, to put it in contemporary terms, were so many Arnold Schwarzeneggers, Roseanne Barrs, and Sylvester Stallones joined into one powerful body. Socialist realism was an optimistic and joyous art. Nowhere else was there so much faith in a bright future and the definitive victory of good over evil.

Nowhere except in market-oriented culture. Most of today's literary production bases its success on the simple socialist-realist idea of progress. Bookstore counters are heaped with books which contain one single idea: how to overcome personal disability, how to improve one's own situation. Books about blind people regaining their sight, fat people becoming thin, sick people recovering, poor people becoming rich, mutes speaking, alcoholics sobering up, unbelievers discovering faith, the unfortunate becoming lucky. All these books infect the reading public with the virus of belief in a bright personal future. And a bright personal future is at the same time a bright collective future, as Oprah Winfrey unambiguously suggests to her impressive world audience.

To be successful, market literature must be didactic. Hence the enormous number of books with the word "How" in their titles. *How to* this and *How to* that—*How the Steel Was Tempered*. The American best-seller *How Stella Got Her Groove Back* has roughly the same healing effect on the American black oppressed female proletariat as Maxim Gorky's novel *Mother* once had on the Soviet one.

Contemporary market literature is realistic, optimistic, joyful, sexy, explicitly or implicitly didactic, and intended for the broad reading masses. As such, it ideologically remolds and educates the working people in the spirit of personal victory, the victory of some good over some evil. It is socialist realist.

Some seventy years have passed since the birth of socialist realism. East European writers are the ones who lost out in this story—they're the ones I am sorry for—because they lacked the self-confidence to stand up for their own art, and threw the old, hard-working socialist realist writers in the trash without learning from them the skills they need in the literary marketplace. They battered their child to death.

And so, socialist realism is dead. Long live socialist realism!

1996

You Know a Craftsman by His Tools

The contemporary book market warmly supports the democratic idea that everyone can be a writer. It derives a significant profit from both the idea and the practice, because anyone can be a writer, but a craftsman needs tools.

This, at least, is what is suggested by those numerous books that instruct the potential writer in how to succeed with his own bare talent. The diverse "do-it-yourself" market also serves established writers—when writing is in question, there is always something to be learned. For instance, *12 Things I Wish I Had Known When I Started Writing*.

The beginner starts with the books that provide information about the market for each particular genre—for instance, *The Novel and Short Story Writer's Market*. Then he learns where and how to sell his manuscript *(Getting Published: What Every Writer Needs to Know)*. After that, there are books that instruct freelance writers on how to make money *(Making Money, Freelance Writing)*. For impatient and greedy writers, there are books for developing effective work habits, for pulling in better fees, and for learning the tricks of the trade *(Write More, Sell More)*. Those who don't believe in instant success can turn to *Writing Fiction Step by Step*.

The beginner should consult *Guide to Getting Started in Writing*, as well as *How to Write and Sell Your First Novel*, a book with sound instructions about writing a "powerful manuscript."

The assumption that talent is not equally distributed in every individual, and that every writer has his strengths and weaknesses, has driven the market to help here as well. If the writer has trouble with dialogue, it wouldn't be a bad idea to browse through *Writing Dialogue*. If he gets stuck on creating characters, maybe *Creating Character Emotions* can help. If he feels that his characters are still flat, there is a book called *Building Believable Characters*. If his characters are emotionally cold and unconvincing, they can at least be dynamic, as he can discover in the book *Dynamic Characters*. However, if the writer wants his characters to be sensitive and convincing and dynamic all at the same time, then he should certainly turn to *How to Write Characters Readers Love*.

If the writer feels that he has completely mastered the art of character, but that his fiction lacks real tension, then he ought to buy *The Art of Compelling Fiction*. The author of this book guarantees to reveal which key components make an ordinary story into an unforgettable one. If the writer feels that he is not excessively gifted in descriptions, he might find it useful to check out *Word Painting: A Guide to Writing More Descriptively*. If the writer thinks that his prose is getting fat, then he should do something about it. *Dictionary of Concise Writing* tells writers how to keep their fiction as thin and crispy as fat free potato chips.

In the literary market there are different kinds of writers, different genres, and an infinite repertoire of themes which can hardly wait to fall into talented hands. There are books about that as well. No writer inclined to science fiction can very well start writing before having read *Aliens and Alien Societies*. For writers more inclined to ordinary life, there is *Writing Life Stories*. The market is inundated with books which instruct the writer how to write from the heart *(Writing Articles from the Heart: How to Write and Sell Your Life Experience)* and how to buy and sell one's own life *(Writing from Personal Experience: How to Turn Your Life into Saleable Fiction)*.

There are lots of books about all sorts of interesting things: how to build a story line *(20 Master Plots and How to Build Them)*, how to write detective stories *(The Writer's Complete Crime Reference Book)*, romances *(Writing Romances)*, Christian novels *(Writing and Selling Christian Novels)*, historical novels *(Write True-to-Life Historical Fiction)*, children's stories, travel stories, and screenplays.

There are also specialist magazines, with instructive supplements about how to begin a novel and how to end it, where to find characters and how to write best-sellers *(How to Finish Your Novel; How to Discover Your Characters; 12 Steps to a Best-Seller; Finding and Shaping Story Ideas; A 5-Point Plan for Creating Great Characters; 7 Must-Haves for a Great Article).*

There are instructional tapes and videos, courses, workshops, and therapists for those in whom the writer is locked and simply can't get out. Therapists advertise their services with slogans such as "We can free the writer in you!" In the diverse American market, there is only one thing it is hard to find: a manual about how to write such manuals.

There are also several series of books for dummies, idiots, and other miscellaneous stupid people. Believing that I belonged to the last category, I bought *The Observation Pack: A Tool Kit for Writers* by Naomi Epel. The author is a "literary escort" by profession, a person who takes care of writers on promotional tours. Although the *Kit* cost twice as much as ordinary manuals ($19.95), I made the investment. Everything exclusive costs money. Besides, a literary escort must be a person of literary knowledge. "Almost every day for the last nine years, I have had a different writer in my car," writes the author of the *Kit*.

A Tool Kit for Writers is a box of stiff cardboard. In the box there are two drawers. In one there is a book, and in the other cards. There are fifty cards, to match the fifty chapters in the manual. On each card there is a message, and the book explains the meaning of each message. Now the tool kit sits on my desk. I practice my craft with my tools.

Every morning I sit down at my desk and shuffle the cards. I lay them out face down. Then I turn the cards over and obediently do as each card instructs.

Consult the News, suggests the card. I go down to the nearest kiosk and buy a newspaper in case I might find an idea for a story there, as the author of the *Kit* suggests. It is precisely in newspapers that many writers, from Truman Capote to Tom Clancy, have found ideas for their stories.

Zoom In and Out, it says on another card. Sitting on my chair, I put my feet on the desk and imagine that I am a camera. I zoom in on my big toe (I need a pedicure!). Then I zoom in on the objects on my desk. As I zoom, I notice many things, for example, that the top shelf is dusty. This exercise sharpens the writer's vision and sense of perspective. I do this exercise for ten minutes.

Observe a Ritual! It turns out that many writers have little rituals they use to start and stop writing. Jack Kerouac used to light a candle before he started to write, Somerset Maugham put on a special hat. My ritual is that every day before I start writing, I turn over five cards from my *Tool Kit for Writers* and do as I'm told.

Breathe! Breathing helps writing, says the author of the *Kit*. Breathing frees the passages so that ideas can circulate freely. It's not a bad idea when breathing to repeat a mantra to oneself. This can be a quotation, a line of verse, a name, nonsense, whatever. I change my mantra according to whatever is preoccupying me at a given time. I breathe and repeat to myself: "Don't forget to pay the phone bill. Don't forget to pay the phone bill." I do this exercise for fifteen minutes.

Switch Media! It turns out that when they are in a crisis or tired, many writers like to switch media. The change helps them find solutions to their creative problems. Leslie Marmon Silko simply could not finish her novel. And then she noticed that she was annoyed by the white wall she had to look at from her window. She went outside, got some paint and brushes, and began to paint the wall. When she finished the mural, the wall was covered by a large brightly colored snake about fifteen feet long with human skulls rolling around in its belly. Leslie returned to her desk and completed her novel just like that. I like to switch media too. When I turn over the *Switch Media!* card, I get out the vacuum cleaner and vacuum the apartment for fifteen minutes.

I have to confess that the card I most like to turn over is the one that says *Take a Walk*. Then I leave my writing and go out for a walk, just as Thornton Wilder, William Saroyan, Thomas Wolfe, Ray Bradbury, Carlos Fuentes, and many other writers used to do. The author of the *Tool Kit for Writers* maintains that when writers take walks they are not wasting time but working. In other words, walking is writing in one's thoughts. That is why I take care not to return from my walk until the end of the working day.

1999

Bazaar

The hall was filled with the brilliant representatives of the female academic and non-academic intelligentsia, mostly American women: writers, professors, artists. They included a well-known expert on spiders (Spider Woman!), several historians, a postcolonial expert on Indonesia, a specialist on the history of China, two mathematicians, a gender-oriented musicologist, two gender-oriented philosophers, an expert on Confucius, a human rights-oriented journalist with an unfinished manuscript about Peru, the author of a manuscript about art and psychoanalysis, a respected expert on the life of seaweed, a well-known lesbian poet, an anthropologist, a well-known expert on the Bushmen, a specialist on dolphins, and even a blind photographer—all in all, some thirty writers of unpublished manuscripts.

The organizers had given us a timetable and instructions. "Don't waste the agents' and editors' precious time! Be prepared to make a quick, concise presentation! You have five minutes to describe your work and ten minutes for a conversation with the editor or agent!"

The editors and agents were sitting in different rooms, with their names hung on the doors. Each of us was given an exact timetable: 2:00 meeting with Mr. X; 2:15 meeting with Ms. Y; 2:30 meeting with Ms. Z.

At precisely the agreed time I appeared in the room of Ms. X, a well-known literary agent.

"You are . . . ?" she said, studying her timetable.

I pronounced my surname.

"Eastern Europe?"

"Yes," I replied concisely. It didn't occur to me to go into geopolitical details.

"What a coincidence," she brightened up, "I'm going to that Eastern Europe of yours in a few days!"

"Where to?" I brightened up as well, quite unreasonably.

"Umm . . . Romania? Or is it Bulgaria? I must check my program," she said warmly.

"Why are you going?" I asked, although I shouldn't have cared.

"Several of us are going . . . publishers and agents. Just to check out the literary scene. Find some young Bulgarian writer. Imagine, at the moment there isn't a single Bulgarian on the market. Do you know any? The most important thing is that he should be young and good-looking!"

"Why? What are you, literary agents or pedophiles?" I burst out.

"Ha ha!" she laughed heartily. "Pedophiles. . . ."

Shaking with laughter, she glanced at her watch and then held out her hand. I held out mine as well. At the same time I looked at my watch. I had two minutes to reach Mr. Y's room.

"Essays, you say."

"Yes," I said as concisely as I could.

"And you say it just like that?"

"What do you mean?"

"I mean, you say that so calmly, as though it were self-explanatory."

"I don't understand. . . ."

"It's as though you were offering me a volume of poetry without a flicker of embarrassment!" the editor said angrily.

"What's wrong with a volume of poetry?"

"What planet do you live on! It doesn't sell, that's what! Hopeless. Just like essays!"

"OK," I said meekly.

"Why don't you turn those essays into nonfiction narrative."

"Into what?"

Then my fellow writer, the expert on Bushmen, came into the room. I left without having discovered what nonfiction narrative was. I had just two minutes to find the room of Ms. Z, the editor. In the corridor I ran into a weeping philosopher.

"How can I squeeze my Confucius into five minutes! How?"

All in all, the bazaar ended cheerfully. The brilliant representatives of the female intelligentsia, academic and non-academic, went down to the reception and fell, starving, upon the crackers, cheese, and white wine. With their mouths full, they described their encounters with the well-known editors and agents. As far as the editors and agents were concerned, they had found their star: the expert on dolphins.

Rachel, the expert on dolphins, told me in passing, "I've spent seventeen years studying dolphins, and now the publishers want me to commercialize my hard-won knowledge. What should I do?"

"Commercialize, Rachel," I said. "Go ahead and commercialize! For the dolphins' sake."

A few days later I met Ellen, the expert on art and psychoanalysis.

"You know," she said, "our bazaar taught me a lot. It may not matter to you, you're from Eastern Europe, but we have to think commercially over here. If you don't, no one's going to publish your book. So I've decided to change my topic. Or at least add a chapter on psychoanalysis and animals. In art, of course. What do you think?"

"You don't need to apologize, Ellen," I said. "After all those meetings, I decided to change the name of my new novel too."

"To what?"

"*All the Dolphins I've Known and Loved!*"

1996

The Market

3 ————————————————

Sometimes he thought sadly to himself, "Why?" and
sometimes he thought, "Wherefore?" and sometimes
he thought, "Inasmuch as which?"—and sometimes
he didn't quite know what he *was* thinking about.

Literature and Democracy

One of the most enduring stereotypes stuck in the heads of citizens of Western democracies is the idea that people in the former communist systems were mere numbers deprived of individual freedom. Now that the communist countries have been shattered like cheap cups, it is time that the stereotypes about them should be broken as well, although stereotypes are the hardest things to throw out. With stereotypes we feel less alone.

Maxim Gorky's slogan—*Man, how proud a sound!*—had more influence on the individual liberation of the East European masses than the French Revolution. Every citizen of a Western democracy who happened to find himself in one of the former totalitarian régimes will admit that there were many things which puzzled him. I presume that restaurants provided his first insight into communist relations. Our Westerner certainly remembers those gloomy waiters who hissed curt replies through clenched teeth while waving a napkin as though they were about to hit their customer with it. Those hours of waiting for the food he had ordered, before eating it, his nerves thoroughly frayed, as though it were the sacred host. The way he wondered in horror why waiters weren't waiters and why a shop assistant (the one who had shouted at him after he had waited patiently in line for three hours) wasn't a shop assistant. Why? Because the idea of the equality of all people in this world is deeply communist and because both the waiter and the shop assistant had drunk in *Man, how proud a sound!* with their mother's milk. I am sure that the waiter was writing a novel at the time, and felt more like a novelist temporarily employed in the catering trade than a waiter, while the shop assistant painted in her spare time, and saw herself as Rembrandt with a job on the side.

In the former Yugoslavia (although maybe it's unfair to use a country that collapsed as an example), there was a Union of Yugoslav Writers and a parallel, properly registered Union of Yugoslav Amateur Writers. The president of that union was an electrician by trade. How do I know? I read one of his novels and greatly enjoyed it.

Today all those countries are practicing postcommunist democracy, as though following a textbook. Waiters are really waiters now; they will polish your shoes for you with the above-mentioned napkin if you need it. It doesn't occur to shop assistants to be rude; on the contrary, they will offer you extra services in their free time, without you even asking.

Meanwhile, the slogan *Man, how proud a sound!* seems to have moved to the West, where it belongs. I find myself watching a TV interview with a prostitute. "I'm not a prostitute, I'm a pleasure activist," says the prostitute. Then I read an interview with Radovan Karadžić, who destroyed the entire city of Sarajevo. "I'm not a monster, I'm a writer," says Karadžić with conviction. On TV I saw that a twelve-year-old child has published a book. "From my earliest childhood, I knew I was going to be a writer," she said confidently.

What can I say, life in the world of literary democracy has seriously shaken my self-esteem. I no longer know what my profession is. I don't know who I am or where to go.

I really don't feel like going to Parnassus. I don't feel like jostling with cooks and electricians there. I have nothing against cooks and electricians, of course. We're all equal—man, whether a cook or an electrician or a writer, is always a proud sound. But Parnassus has become a cheap trade union rest home, and I do have some experience with that kind of collective hedonism. I really don't feel like sharing tinned meat paste and dry bread with some novel-writing chauffeur. And I wouldn't go to that other mountain either, Olympus, even if I were invited. That's where the newfangled gods hang out, mega-writers, literary tycoons, Hollywood Prousts, coddled by the Muses, those zealous employees of the leisure industry.

And then suddenly, in the middle of my identity crisis, I am struck by the realization, like a thunderbolt from the sky, that I am an *activist* and that in fact I have never been anything else. I have spent night after night with Shakespeare, Goethe, Tolstoy just to penetrate the secrets of my future craft. I sweated under James Joyce just to master the most sophisticated literary skills. I went to bed with lots of writers, even Russians, even two writers at once, Ilf and Petrov, to learn the sweet strategies of seduction. I slept with Dumas, Rabelais, and Hašek in order to learn the techniques of achieving literary satisfaction. I spent lots of nights with lots of people and I was up for anything: old men, women, children, gay men. Victor Hugo and Marina Tsvetaeva, Arthur Rimbaud and Oscar Wilde.

When I felt ready, I detached myself from my teachers and set to work. I softened clumsy words with my own saliva in order to stimulate some grumpy literary client. I stripped, writhed, enticed, what didn't I do to force my reader's greasy hand to turn the next page of my book! I tenderly licked and nibbled his ear just to force it, that big fat ear, to prick up and open a passage to the seductive gurgling of my words.

What is that if not activism? I am the real pleasure activist! And I won't let anyone take the dignity of my profession away from me.

1997

Engineers of Human Souls

Literary theory—which is concerned with kinds, types, and genres, structures, models, and patterns; with connotations and denotations, discourses, forms, and formations; with text, metatext, and intertext; with semantics, semiotics, and deconstruction—has hardly ever concerned itself with the specific role of money in the genesis of a literary text. I understand that this isn't its business, but the results of such research might be interesting.

"What made you decide to move from short stories to the novel form?" a well-known contemporary American writer, valued particularly for her short stories, was once asked in an interview.

"A six-figure advance," replied the writer.

A six-figure advance! The answer probably did not surprise anyone. In fact, I bet many people liked her for saying it, because it dispels the fog of mystification around the writer's business. And some would envy her. Me, for example.

The media stood unanimously behind Joan Collins when her publisher sued her for taking a four million dollar advance and not submitting a manuscript in accordance with her agreement with the publisher. Instead of the six murders that had been agreed upon, Joan had added a seventh in her creative enthusiasm. Or something like that. "Was the publisher expecting a new *Ulysses*?" the journalists defended Ms. Collins. The publisher lost the case.

The demands of the market have no ideology; they have been cleansed of it, they are pure, desirable, wreathed in glamour and glory. What the market decides is confirmed by millions, and its moral dimension is not in question. The work is worth as much as we pay for it. Ideological mandates, on the other hand, are seen as seriously discrediting the vocation of literature. But people overlook the fact that both kinds of mandate require the same level of professionalism in the writer.

The former communist, noncommercial cultures, particularly in Stalin's days, must be given credit for the professionalization of the writer's craft. Soviet poets were paid by the line and it is quite possible that the abundance of epic poems had some connection with that fact. Soviet fiction writers were paid by the page and it is quite possible that this detail affected the size of Russian socialist realist novels. Admittedly, literary historians will say that it was a question of attaching the socialist realist novels forcibly to the tradition of nineteenth-century realism, which was one of the main tenets of the Stalinist literary-ideological package, and they are, of course, right. However, the two explanations do not exclude one another, indeed they support each other.

I maintain that Stalinism was a stern school of literary professionalism. Stalinism made writers into professionals, who would surely be rampaging through the international literary market now, if only they'd lived. Writers had to be professionals, it was a matter of life or death. Stalinist writers had to take great care to follow the rules of the game: the rules of socialist realism. And those rules were not only ideological but also commercial. Literature had to be comprehensible to the broad reading masses; there was no place for avant-gardism and the antics of experimentalism. One had to have human and professional nerve to spend time building a dam and turn that into a novel. One had to squelch through a muddy *kolhoz,* and then at the request of some publisher write a novel which would be convincing to the vast Soviet masses. One had to know how to use narrative techniques, to control one's own creative impulses and literary taste, to clench one's teeth and write within the framework of the given norm. Only a true professional could agree to something like that. Writers who were unable to adapt to the demands of the ideological market ended tragically: in camps. Nowadays, writers who cannot adapt to commercial demands end up in their own personal ghetto of anonymity and poverty.

Contemporary commercial professionalism also deals in designated genres. The professional writer knows that no deviation is allowed, that things must develop exactly according to the genre and the expectations of the broad reading public. He knows that every deviation increases the risk of failure and that regular testing of the pulse of the literary genre increases the chances of success. Today's romances, "hospital" novels, "horror" novels, "Hollywood" novels, and other such popular novels are only commercial variations on the old socialist-realist "production" novel. In short, if Stephen King had found himself in Stalinist Russia, he would undoubtedly have gotten the Stalin Prize.

That much mocked Stalinist catch-phrase for writers, *engineers of human souls,* sounds quite appropriate for today's mass-production writers. Engineers work in factories, don't they? Who works in the publishing *industry?* Tender souls visited by muses, or industrial workers, including, presumably, engineers?

Stephen King is just one of the numerous modern engineers of human souls. This mega-writer got a mega-advance of seventeen million dollars for his latest book. The communist soul engineers would get an advance on their future historical guilt, crates of vodka, cirrhosis of the liver, and the constant possibility of a knock on the door from the KGB.

Ideology: that's where high-caliber professionals were tempered. The market: that's where high-caliber professionals are tempered. Those writers who compromised the honor of the literary muse are now dead: Fadeev, Gladkov, Furmanov. . . . Who remembers their names now? They were losers in their lifetimes and they have remained losers after their death. A thick layer of dust has settled on their books. But today's commercial ones are alive and famous. Their influence is planetary. They are respected. It is hard not to respect the figures of their mega-advances.

That is why it is fitting to give the old Stalinist writers due credit for their devoted work toward the development of literary professionalism, for anticipating commercial principles in literature, for their dedication in capturing the vast reading masses. It is fitting finally to take off our hats to them, those masters of their craft, those engineers of the human soul.

1997

The Writer as Literary Reference

Some time ago I read an interview with a writer, call her X. The most important thing, she suggested, was to become *an unavoidable literary reference*. X has, it must be said, a second-rate talent, but with the vigorous intelligence of a stockbroker and in her immediate say-whatever-comes-into-your-mind foolishness, she had spoken a great, contemporary literary truth. Meanwhile, X really had become an unavoidable literary reference.

"Life is a constant struggle between good and evil, as the writer X once put it so wonderfully and profoundly. What is life for you?" I was once asked by a journalist.

I didn't dare ask the journalist whether he had anything from Walter Benjamin's repertoire of quotations. I would have felt more confident with Mr. Benjamin. As it was, I was obliged to comment on the *wonderful and profound* thought of X. I could, of course, have refused, but that would not have been wise. Why? Because on the stormy literary ocean, I too was rowing towards the point of salvation known as *becoming an unavoidable literary reference*.

In order to become an unavoidable literary reference, a writer must be born with the belief that this is what he will one day become. Only this faith gives him *that* facial expression and *that* kind of walk (as though dozens of TV cameras were focused on him), which are hard to imitate. Such things come with a high degree of self-confidence. And everywhere, including in the literary marketplace, a high degree of self-confidence is half the battle.

To become a literary reference, it is best to make use of—literary references. The blurb is one of these devices, only apparently innocent. If words such as *fantastic, astonishing, powerful, a real feast, stunningly moving, marvelous, entertaining, amusing, wry, ingenious, lucid, subtle, beautiful, absorbing, fascinating, illuminating, inspiring, challenging,* and so on accompany the name of some well-known person on the back of your own book, entrance to the world of references is almost guaranteed. And the well-known person need not be a writer. Bill Gates and Madonna are more effective promoters than Günter Grass.

A contemporary Yugoslav writer wrote a novel which, through some error in market calculations, became an international best-seller. The writer believed his success in the literary lottery was his literary-historical due and he set about publishing a book of blurbs he had accumulated as a best-selling writer. Now that book is a unique literary shrine, if not to the writer, then certainly to the Holy Blurb itself.

If he wishes to enter the world of references, a writer must be open, accessible, and communicative, in other words he must go wherever he is invited. In addition, such a writer must learn, at least in the prereferential phase (if he is not naturally gifted), to pronounce easily memorable banalities that will be preserved in the storehouses of so-called eternal truths: the dictionaries of quotations. The interview is usually the most effective way for a writer to offer his potential reader the democratic opportunity to be lifted with him into the spheres of the spirit. The spheres of the spirit need not necessarily be particularly high. That is, the warmer a writer is and the more comprehensible, the more he will be loved. And quoted. And only writers who are quoted become references. In fact, it's difficult to quote good writers. Quotations from bad writers are more transparent. However, even good writers know their profession. Masters of their craft deliberately sprinkle their works with sentences suitable for quotation. The writer, the future reference, knows that the contemporary literary world is not divided into good and bad writers, but into the writer-references and the anonymous.

So what changes when a writer becomes a literary reference? Nothing, apart from the fact that only a literary reference has become a writer in the full sense of the word. Because no one wants to take on the thankless task of evaluating the writer-reference. The writer-reference is hardly read by editors, hardly read by critics, hardly read by other writer-references, hardly read even by the people who give him prizes. To be a writer-reference means to have diplomatic immunity in the literary world, to possess indisputable, unquestioned literary authority. It also means to live on the income pouring in from one's inexhaustible account of referentiality. The writer-reference becomes a suitable person to write blurbs for other writers (without reading their books) and thus increase his own rating. The writer-reference becomes an unavoidable name in anthologies, both national and international anthologies (when the editors have to find a name or two for a given national literature), and an unavoidable name in course readers and syllabi. To be a writer-reference means to have a ticket to eternity, and the writer's eternity is called literary history. And what is the history of literature if not a history of literary references?

A little while ago I set out with some trepidation to check my rating in the world of references. It turned out that I had no cause for concern. The Internet spat out a decent number of items connected with my name. What can I say, I felt like a real reference. I was one of twenty or so bibliographic references in the C.V. of a literary critic from Athens, Ohio. My reading was one of fifty or so events in the semester schedule of a school which I had once visited without any inkling that my audience were experts in surfing the net. I was one of a hundred or so references in the impressive web page of a TV critic, I was one of two hundred references in a book about the war in the Balkans, and one among three hundred references in another book about the war in the Balkans.

And I quickly understood. When I catapult myself into cyberspace, they will all be references on my web page too. That is how we assure ourselves eternal life. Because only people are mortal. We are something else, we are references. The only thing that can spoil our eternal life is the inflation of unavoidable literary references. But until that time comes, Google me, baby, and I'll Google you back. . . .

1997

The Aura of Glamour

For some reason I recently remembered poor Dr. Barnard, the heart transplant expert, who flashed onto the public scene in the '70s and then vanished. His example demonstrates that, with the best will in the world, many professions do not have sufficient star potential. The essence of star potential consists of the conviction of the broad masses that they too, each and every one of them, could be in the media star's place, given just a little luck in their lives. In Dr. Barnard's case, the disenfranchised masses condemned to anonymity quickly realized that although they could all be patients, not all of them could be surgeons, and Dr. Barnard stepped down from his starry path, withdrawing into professional anonymity. The aura of glamour is, it seems, reserved only for those public activities which create the illusion that everyone has the same access to it.

In the contemporary media market, literature too has acquired an aura of glamour. How has it come about that all sorts of people are now rushing into the places formerly reserved for outsiders, bookworms, romantics, and losers? What is so attractive about the literary profession today that it makes so many people mill around the marketplace awaiting their starry moment? Money? Perhaps. But then why do even financially secure movie stars rush to try their hand at a children's book or novel, in addition to the autobiography which is expected of them? Why do serious people—literary theoreticians, psychologists, doctors—do the same thing?

51

In a November 1997 issue of the *Guardian,* there was a barbed correspondence between the art critic David Lee and Tracey Emin, a successful young artist and gallery owner. Lee dared to say that most modern artistic creation was the result of a "confidence trick," and accused young artists above all of illiteracy. The young woman responded to his accusation by snapping back: "What if I am illiterate? I still have the right to a voice!"

The young artist's answer contains a basic assumption of the contemporary art industry. In the democratic marketplace everyone has a right to his or her artistic voice. For centuries, with rare exceptions, art has been reserved for the "literate," but today the market opens its doors to everyone. Indeed, the artistically "illiterate" are often more commercially successful than the artistically "literate."

But still, is that the only reason why so many try their hand in the artistic marketplace? Despite the fact that "everyone can do it," art has, quite paradoxically, retained its aura of exclusivity. The field of art creates among other things the illusion that, if we end up there, we can stay forever. We have written graffitti on the wall—a book—and who knows, maybe by that very act we have already engraved our name in the indifferent honor roll of eternity.

The market has destroyed the closed artistic institutions, the academies and faculties; has trampled underfoot the old-fashioned artistic arbiters, the "guardians of good taste," the theoreticians of art and literature; has dismissed the stern and demanding critics, steamrolled the prevailing aesthetic scales of values and built its own cast-iron commercial-aesthetic criteria. For example: what sells is good, what doesn't sell is bad. Many are attracted by that simple commercial formula, seeing in it a chance for themselves. The old communist utopia, in which art is created and consumed by everyone, has been transformed by the modern market into a possible reality.

Realizing that they have been deprived forever of their position as protected losers, writers have radically changed their image. Tubercular neurotics, humble bunglers, drunks, wastrels, bohemians, thin men and women in black wool sweaters leaning against a well-stocked home bookshelf, bearded intellectuals in tweed jackets with academic patches on the elbows and books in their hands, short-sighted smokers of pipes and cigars—they are all a thing of the distant past.

Although the publishing industry describes writers as "content providers," their work is more than that. They are also image providers. These days, writers are increasingly adapting their images to the content of their books and the content of their books to their image. So S. M., a current American literary star, has had herself photographed in a transparent white dress standing in the doorway of a sleazy toilet. The photograph explains the basic content of the novel, the photograph is a visual blurb, but it is more than that: it feeds the reader's imagination by suggesting that she, the writer herself, not her main character, could be the real heroine of the dark erotic activities described in the novel.

Resigned to the cruel laws of the marketplace, women writers submit to face-lifts, justifying themselves by saying that their profession demands it of them. In their photographs, male writers increasingly display intelligently formed muscles and bare their shaggy chests. They are all regularly photographed with a self-confident "I know what I want" expression. In the short biographies on book jackets, no one mentions the year of their birth, but they happily include morally correct details from their private lives with a spouse and two children. If they are physically attractive, their photograph appears on the book's cover. The photograph aims at the age of the readers: authors try to remain young for as long as possible so that their image can appeal to the broadest possible age range of potential readers. Their acknowledgments mention—in addition to husbands and wives, editors, agents, friends, and inspirers—their beloved cats or dogs, in order to appeal to an audience of animal lovers.

Milan Kundera wrote that one day, when everyone writes, nobody will listen. The market, it seems, is creating that utopia. But nevertheless, in the whole commercial whirligig, there is a sad and paradoxical truth: glamour is a populist longing, a sign of absence. Literacy can have an aura of glamour only where literacy does not exist.

And in connection with the evident end of a literary period, it is hard not to recall Kundera's compatriot, Bohumil Hrabal. There is a photograph of

Hrabal in which the old man is wearing a completely inappropriate Scottish golfer's cap. Although it was taken only a few years ago, this photograph seems to belong to some distant literary age. Hrabal recently passed into the other world. They say that he fell out of a Prague hospital window as he was stretching out his old man's hand to feed the pigeons. Whatever actually happened, Hrabal did not think that he had any particular right to his *own* voice. Perhaps this was because that was just what his voice was—his *own*.

1997

Shares in Human Perversion

Nowadays the notorious Marquis de Sade reads like a children's writer. I tested this when I picked him up recently and giggled as though I were being tickled, as though I were reading one of my favorite writers from early childhood. The juicy Molly Bloom is a housewife amusing herself by spending hours poeticizing her own orgasm, a technical affair that no longer interests anyone. Her famous stream of consciousness reads today like instructions for turning on a washing machine, instructions drawn out for fifty pages. Erica Jong's global best-seller, which played an important role in the sexual liberation of the exploited female proletariat, is no longer taken off the library shelf even by old women in retirement homes. Hearty sex full of good intentions seems to occupy the lowest place in the entire history of literary themes. And what is increasing in value with dizzying speed are shares in themes of human perversion.

Writers have become quite feverish with this sudden surge on the literary stock exchange; they compete to invent the most sinister or shocking story. At the same time, human perversion is only incidentally linked to sex. Perversions now appear in novels as individualized entities of their own, almost the main characters of their novels, devoid of passion and pleasure, real reason, energy, and will, devoid of drama, alienated from both their perpetrators and their victims.

So some players on the stock exchange trade in cannibalism. A novel recently appeared in which the urban main character uses her lover for gastronomic purposes. The novel is perfectly adapted to the contemporary image of modern woman and modern evil. The modern man-eating woman is alienated from her cultural history. There is no indication that she has any cultural-historical connection with the licentious Bacchae, nor that she knows the pleasure with which Balkan people, those descendants of the Bacchae, still sink their teeth into humanoid animals, into roast ox on the spit, into an ox's stomach filled with finely chopped offal, into a roast sheep's head, out of which they lasciviously suck the large, sad eyes like efficient little vacuum cleaners. The cannibalism of the urban man-eating woman is adapted to her times, it is low-fat and low-cholesterol, a little dietary treat in her lunch hour. The modern man-eater will consume her lover like Japanese sushi. That is why she devours not what any "normal" reader would first think of, but something quite different. And if we follow the logic of the lover's cannibalism which has been imposed on us, then, for that little piece of fresh, sexually indifferent meat—a mere piece from the palm of his hand—it was hardly worth killing a whole man.

Societies for the prevention of cruelty to human beings are hard to come by, but the ever-vigilant societies for the prevention of cruelty to animals often drop the ball as well. They should by all rights have protested against a book which advocates the cruel and unusual feeding of fish, but I have yet to hear that they did. The instance I mean is the novel currently flooding American and European bookstores, about a teacher of creative writing who becomes involved with a couple of policemen. One of them is a passionate fisherman who has hit on the idea of using women's nipples as bait, so that the teacher ends up as bait, which is, of course, not without a certain titillating metaphorical appeal. Many readers' fish have been caught with this bait. Not even the stern German literary critics could resist declaring this the book of the year.

While women writers are still obsessed with the oral phase (eating someone or being eaten), male writers are more inclined to the anal. Novels about child abuse, sadists, and all kinds of perverts who snap fragile children's bodies are at a high premium.

The list of contemporary artists who are exciting the market with shocking projects is too long. Filmmakers compete with writers, visual artists with filmmakers. When it comes to the market, no one shrinks from anything, everything is welcome, even the peace-loving domestic animals which are currently being sexually abused for artistic purposes by the Russian artist Oleg Kulik.

And while thousands of little Nepalese girls, whose parents sell them to brothels in Bombay for the price of a transistor radio, are dying of AIDS because men infected with AIDS believe that sex with a virgin will cure them, contemporary writers struggle to dream up masterpieces of child abuse. And while contemporary writers struggle to dream up some original perversity, ordinary criminal brains, with far lower IQs, easily outdo them in inventiveness and creativity. Miro B., member of a Croatian paramilitary group with the poetic name Autumn Rain, made a public confession in which he listed everything he had done to the hated Serbs. He burned them with a flame from a gas cylinder, poured vinegar over their genitals and eyes and attached them to electric cables, hammered nails under their fingernails, switched on high voltage power and turned them to ash, which, he admitted, he had not thought up himself, "although he knew Lenz's law." In another recent public confession, a criminal with the picturesque nickname of Cannon, a member of a Serbian paramilitary group, listed everything he had done to the hated Muslims. Among other things, he had cut off their left ears (but only of those he had "personally killed," he said that he didn't want to "adorn himself with someone's else's feathers"). Then he sold his trophies, a little surprised by the fact that there were people who would buy such things. ("People want to own a Muslim ear!") Both of them remark on the development of the real-life story line: "The first time is the hardest, after that it's easy."

No one is interested in real victims, or real criminals. Not local courts, not their fellow citizens, not publishers, and not readers. Everyone simply refuses to believe them. An imaginary crime is more convincing; reality is too real. They can only identify with an invented crime, only paper evil can excite them. We can easily imagine a contemporary reader sitting in pools of real blood, on a heap of real bodies, reading a novel about human perversion with rapt attention. Even for those who are resigned to the idea that literature is dead, such a scene must restore their hope. How can one not be amazed by the magical power of the written word!

1997

Eco among the Nudists

At 25, I first stood naked in front of an audience. Was I embarrassed? I don't know. Art was stronger.—Interview with a well-known contemporary artist

About twenty years ago, I spent my summer vacation on an island in the Adriatic. The next, uninhabited island was occupied by tourists of a nudist inclination. The only way to that island was by a little boat, driven by a local man. One day, out of curiosity to see the little island, I asked the man to take me over. As we approached the island, the naked bodies scattered over the rocks became increasingly visible. A little later, roaming over the island to find a place for myself, I noticed that all those naked bodies were holding a book in their hands. The *same* book, but in several different languages. The author of the book was Umberto Eco and its title was *The Name of the Rose*.

As far as one could see, the naked bodies belonged neither to intellectuals (who are generally reluctant to go to the beach), nor to the wealthy (it was generally tourists of relatively slender means who came to the Adriatic). The readers of Eco's novel could have been German cooks, Italian typists, Austrian workers, Swiss schoolteachers, Dutch bus drivers, Hungarian butchers, Czech civil servants, and English pensioners. I wondered how the renowned professor of semiotics had become the summer reading of a cook, a secretary, a teacher, a bus driver, a butcher, and a civil servant. I also wondered whether my assumptions about contemporary readers had gotten stuck in the intellectual stereotype that cooks read romances if they read at all. And I wondered where the naked readers' enthusiasm came from. Personally, drained by the strong sun, I had no energy for anything, let alone for Umberto Eco.

And then at a certain point, I turned full circle and was suddenly filled with a new, exciting faith in literature. These naked bodies scattered over the Arcadian space of a small Adriatic island were reading books! The bodies could have been having sex, yawning, picking their noses, scratching their asses, munching sandwiches while pulling the skins of unpeeled local salami out of them, snoring, looking around, they could have been doing all sorts of things, but they weren't. They were each reading a book! Touched by this naked literary enthusiasm, ashamed of my own mistrust, I relaxed, I found a place on a remote rock and, taking care that no one could see, I took a book out of my bag. The only one I had taken on vacation with me. *The Three Musketeers,* that's what I always take on vacation. But still, because of my sense of personal incompatibility with the nudist readers, I didn't manage to read a single page. So I went back to my own island on the first available boat.

What is the secret of the best-seller, that collective fascination with one book? That is the question which preoccupies writers who have never found themselves on that list, writers who have but don't know how, as well as publishers, editors, critics, followers of literary trends, bookstore owners. Publishers, who believe that they know the secret, are still far too often surprised at how wrong their calculations are. Maybe the secret is simpler than it seems. Best-sellers are bought by everybody: by those who believe in the justice of the readers' majority choice and those who don't, whether they buy the book to test once again their own powers of cultural analysis or simply to see what everyone else is buying. People say that writing a best-seller is like winning the lottery, but this is a lie like the lie of professional gamblers who insist that everything is a matter of luck. Even the naive know that, as well as luck, you have to have money to invest. And the more you invest, the greater your chance of winning. Along with the always stable demand for cookbooks, gardening books, thrillers, and romances, along with individual authors who have their reliable million-strong readership, along with books whose huge print runs do not surprise anyone, there also exists the book which appears like a comet in the literary sky, flares, leaves a million-strong readership breathless, and vanishes. But what exactly a best-seller is remains a mystery.

As an inquisitive follower of literary circumstances, a measurer of literary water levels, I tried for a long time to discover the secret of literary mega-tricks. Until one day the distant image of the little Adriatic island flashed before my eyes together with the thought that there must be a secret connection between the phenomenon of nudism and the phenomenon of the best-seller. I took out a pencil and paper and noted down what I thought about nudists and what I knew about best-sellers.

Nudists try to perform the naturalness that the whole human race lost long ago—in that sense nudists are consciously naive. Nudists are asexual and passionless (only people devoid of passion could calmly stroll around naked!). Nudists are dogmatists of the body, people devoid of irony and humor (it is hard to imagine an ironic nudist). Nudists perform their ideology collectively (an individual nudist would be considered a pervert). Nudists turn existing social norms on their heads with an expression of righteous seriousness on their faces. Nudists are successful manipulators and alchemists, for behind nudist nakedness, that ideology of the absence of ideology, there is a whole series of values which have somehow attached themselves to nudism and seem to be implicit in the whole affair. Nudism implies pacifism (naked and unarmed!), family values (nudists always move in family formations), enlightenment (a naked body is a healthy and moral body), advanced ecological awareness (nature does not pollute nature!), goodness and sincerity (a naked person cannot have ulterior motives!), faith in the righteousness of the divine order (we are naked as God made us!), harmony and innocence (like Adam and Eve in the Garden of Eden), obedience and anti-intellectualism (Adam and Eve were innocent and naked until they bit into the apple from the tree of knowledge).

Likewise, in the phenomenon of the best-seller, there is an element of ritual. If one book is read by millions of readers, it is a kind of substitute for the host (millions stick out their tongues in order to receive a surrogate of the spiritual and thus participate in a collective act of purification). The phenomenon of the best-seller is a projection of the collective longing for one book, for the *book of books,* for a substitute Bible. The longing for one book is deeply anti-intellectual (let us recall that the history of culture begins with tasting that apple from the tree of knowledge!). The best-seller is a space of ritualized collective innocence (we enjoy something which everyone enjoys). The phenomenon of the best-seller contains a manipulative, fascist streak, for the best-seller is a holy marriage between the text and the readers, it is always an ideology, a surrogate of the spiritual. The best-seller offers a closed system of simple values and even simpler knowledge.

I am not a nudist, but this summer I took another trip to the same little Adriatic island to test the accuracy of my literary hypothesis. At the very end of the millennium, the naked bodies were holding in their hands three titles by the same author: Paulo Coelho, the Brazilian writer whose 12 books have been translated into 39 languages and published in 74 countries. In view of the sudden fall in Adriatic tourism because of the war, the naked bodies were on the whole either local or German. So the books bore the titles *Der Alchemist* (a novel which sold 9.5 million copies), *Der Fünfte Berg,* and *Am Ufer des Rio Pedra sass ich und weinte.*

And so I stepped onto the island, naked, compatible, and with a triumphant expression on my face, which came from the realization that my hypothesis was correct. I had not managed to buy *The Alchemist,* Madonna's favorite read, the text from which the mega-star "draws her spiritual energy." And therefore I held in my hand, like a holy cross, Coehlo's *Valkyries,* in the English translation.

I settled myself on a rock and tried to match my own reader's pulse to the global pulse of the literary mega-market. I opened Coehlo's book. A Brazilian married couple in search of the spiritual travels through the American desert (equipped with a book called *The Desert Survival Manual*). In the desert it is of course unbearably hot, so the man and woman take their clothes off and roam around naked (!) in the hope of finding what they have come for, the spiritual. I stopped reading at the place where the man and the woman become dehydrated (because they were naked) and take turns running to the bathroom and vomiting.

"Readers have their own experience, I am not teaching them anything, I am only telling them stories I know," Coehlo modestly said somewhere. This writer with "the soul of a child," this "warrior of the light," has just completed his new novel, *Veronika Decides to Die,* the action of which takes place this time in healthier conditions, in Slovenia.

I closed the book and gazed at the sky. The sky was blue, the clouds calm and white. ("The clouds are rivers that already know the sea," writes Coehlo.) My hypothesis has been confirmed! Nudists and the alchemists of literary success are definitely in some secret concord! Nothing could spoil my sense of victory at this discovery. Not even the thought that Eco, some twenty years earlier, must have been a mistake, a case of dysfunction, an unpredictable literary arrhythmia in the mega-pulse of the literary market.

I reflected on how many publishers would be grateful to me when I published my discovery! How many writers, those poor creatures who spend their lives vainly racking their brains over the alchemy of the best-seller, would thank me! Although so far I had been able to hear only the applause of the noisy island cicadas, I was sure of myself, I was calm as a cloud, which was a river that already knew the sea, I was spiritually nourished like Madonna. Not even a momentary stab of doubt could disturb my tranquility. For "you have to listen to your own heart. It knows everything. Follow its beats even when they lead you into sin," says Coehlo. I was calm, for I knew that the real applause was still to come.

1998

Come Back, Cynics, All Is Forgiven!

I saw a documentary on TV about the way the market is trying to capture New Guinea. Papuan salesmen performed skits in the jungle for their rapturous compatriots, explaining what Coca-Cola was and what Omo detergent was for. The Papuan audience was doubled up with laughter. As I watched the documentary, I laughed as well, with the Papuans.

In conversations I more and more often catch a puzzled expression on the other person's face, an eyebrow raised questioningly, a slight frown on the brow. I am increasingly obliged to stop and add a footnote. "I was joking. Sorry. . . ."

There are only two possible causes of these misunderstandings:

a) I have changed, alas, and I am slowly moving towards the pathetic prospect of an old age spent making boorish and foolish social gaffes;

b) I have not changed, but the world around me has, so my message increasingly misses its target, or at least so it seems to me.

Both possibilities equally threaten my relation to the world. And if that relation is not improved, my position may soon become completely isolated.

It is true that I come from a culture of crude, discriminatory humor, from a culture of duality and duplicity (submission to the authorities and at the same time an underhand skepticism towards any authority), from a culture of paradox and ambivalence, from a culture with a false bottom and fingers crossed behind its back, a culture which has developed strategies in its struggle for survival, just as all people have. I learned how to recognize those strategies, I developed a reflex of mental caution. I come from a culture which, in the choice between diligent work at a desk and sharpening the tongue in a café, always prefers the latter (irony, wit, and cheap jokes). I come from a culture which is recognized more for its cultural outbursts than for its continuity. I come from an aggressive and exclusive, but also paradoxically elastic culture, which keeps harping on its thousand-year past but at the same time changes things with astonishing ease: it destroys its own monuments and libraries, builds roads over Roman ruins, keeps garbage cans in Diocletian's palace. A naive person, unburdened by cultural prejudices, could conclude that I come from the epicenter, the very heart of postmodern culture. And they would be wrong, but at the same time (why not?) equally right.

Perhaps it is because of this cultural environment that I have developed a kind of advantage. I am more sensitive to the disappearance of cultural treasures, which of course makes sense: things have constantly been taken from me, destroyed or paved over, including my mother tongue. And ecology as a discipline came into being where the environment was most destroyed.

I am not, unfortunately, a Papuan. I have mastered the cultural references of this part of the world. I drink Coca-Cola, Omo has foamed in my washing machine, and I have read Shakespeare. So why do I increasingly feel called upon in communication with a reader or an acquaintance to add explanations and apologies?

In his book *Cynicism and Postmodernity,* Timothy Bewes maintains that the phenomenon of sincerity is one of the cultural obsessions of our time. At the beginning of the 1990s, the media, measuring the pulse of the market and picking up a longing for semantic transparency, repackaged the postmodern zeitgeist as the age of honesty. Thus, concludes Bewes, "sincerity has replaced wit and subtlety as the mark of commercial credibility." Ever since the market gave the green light, a heap of products has fallen onto the political, cultural, and media market stalls "whose premise is nothing other than the assertion of their own authenticity." Politicians, the media, pop musicians, artists, writers, and ordinary people all bow to the ideology of authenticity and sincerity. We stumble everywhere over tried, pure, natural, high quality, hundred-percent authenticity, the real thing, real life, real drama.

As an occasional literature professor, I was at first touched by the naive concern of my students to know whether what was described in some work of literature *really* happened or whether it was *just invented*. Among many of them I detected a lack of understanding of the fundamental assumptions of a literary text, an inability to differentiate literary strategies and narrative masks, and a deafness to irony—either they did not understand it, or they considered it morally, politically, fundamentally unacceptable. Then I noticed a reaction which Bewes defines as "a gastric aversion to the cultural products of postmodernism," even a basic aversion to texts which demand effort in their reading and which are, therefore, not "sincere."

Now, some years later, if I look around me, I see that I am buried under cultural products which represent the same values that my students advocated. My surroundings are dominated by the culture of public confession, where the television has taken over the role of the church, and the role of church confessors is played by popular TV presenters. Memoirs are no longer reserved for those who have climbed the Himalayas or swum the Atlantic. On the contrary, what is valued are the *ordinary* accounts of *ordinary* people about *ordinary* things. The market is swamped with products which claim *reality*—from soap operas, which people believe more than life itself, to real-life stories, which people believe as much as soap operas. In the culture of public confession, everyone has acquired the right to his personal fifteen minutes, just as Andy Warhol predicted. The only thing that puzzles me, in this ardent return to reality, is reality itself.

That is, the reality so aggressively offered to me as authentic is in fact soapified reality, a kind of "life for beginners," and it often reminds me of the primitive theatricality of the salesmen in the documentary about the Papuans. The only difference is that the Papuans rocked with laughter. The contents of cheaply literarized reality are those with which the majority identifies, confirming their relevance (the way we were beaten and molested in our childhood, the fact that our father was an alcoholic, that we were ourselves, that we were left by our partners, that we changed jobs, became ill and cured ourselves, found a partner, brought up children . . .). That reality of majority choice is not devoid of its optimistic, positive projection which suggests that when we resolve all these difficulties, we will earn the right to lifelong harmony.

Mainstream culture, about which the sophisticated speak with contempt, has gradually vacuumed up every cultural subversion, including the contempt of the sophisticated, and become simply culture. From the culture of camp, via the postmodern, ironic artistic obsession with bad art, bad art has become art itself. Thanks to the powerful cultural market, "bad" has been transformed into the positively valued "BAD" (Paul Fussell).

In our post–Cold War world, which tends towards globalization and non-conflict, the newly established rules of political correctness and respect for cultural differences wipe away "friction," resistance, ambivalence, cynicism, irony, and the possibility of revolt in the same way. They remove the space for the simple question: Is everything really like that?

The world chooses its gurus accordingly. The living Oprah is a mega-metaphor for the contemporary fetishization of spontaneity and sincerity. The dead Di is the melancholy mega-metaphor of a world tired of jogging towards a better future, which has decided instead to find temporary solace in what is always left to oneself: private life. The heart instead of the mind, sincerity instead of deceit, simplicity instead of sophistication, weakness instead of strength, compassion instead of selfishness. Di has sprinkled the entire world with the stardust of her media aura.

Even the Croatian Minister of Defense, having happily avoided the Hague Tribunal, was buried to the song "Candle in the Wind." In Croatia, as in some other East European countries, sincerity and authenticity are interpreted as a return to the national roots (authenticity as a new fascism). The yes-sayers have chosen to live as authentically "themselves," with their authentically "own kind," having first cleansed the country of inauthentic elements: others, minorities, non-like thinkers and traitors. Inauthentic communism has been replaced by natural, authentic nationalism, so "authentic" that in many places in former Eastern Europe you can now find graffiti with the cry: "Come back, communists, all is forgiven!"

Coca-Cola, "the real thing," has existed for a full hundred years. It was born the same year as the Statue of Liberty. When I think of that fact, it seems to me that the era of "respect," "sincerity," and "authenticity" is likely to last a very long time. Perhaps the performance of sincerity will last until we all show each other pieces of our own fresh heart. An avant-garde gesture of cultural resistance no longer seems possible. We are no longer capable of giving "a slap in the face of public taste." Nor, indeed, is there any firm and clear face to which we could administer it.

Recently, I gave a reading. I was among "my own kind." The audience consisted not only of people acquainted with artistic techniques, but also their practitioners: artists and writers. I read a little darkly humorous story. Had they been able to hear me, Alfred Jarry and Daniil Kharms would have been proud. As it was, the evening was a fiasco. No one in the audience so much as giggled. On the contrary, the story made them all sad. Someone said that my text was a powerful allegory of the recent Yugoslav war. And everyone agreed.

"Ah well," a compatriot consoled me, "it seems that from now on, at least for the foreseeable future, we are condemned to noble suffering. . . ."

So there we are. Because of all of this, I decided to give in. Authentically crushed by the mega-death of Lady Di, hooked for consolation to the mega-show of living Oprah, with the latest mega-best-seller in my hand, voluntarily plugged into the pulse of the world, I send out feeble SOS signals with the remaining subversive millimeter of my brain. Come back, cynics, all is forgiven!

1997

The Role of Kirk Douglas in My Life

I was born in a country that no longer exists, in Yugoslavia, exactly a year after Tito uttered his historic "No" to Stalin (at least that's what we were taught). I was conceived, therefore, at a significant moment, at a moment when a historic "No" was being pronounced. It is possible that this historical moment determined my character. Instead of becoming a cheerful and obedient yes-sayer, I became a bad-tempered no-sayer. I'm even proud of it.

The historic "No" to Stalin meant a historic "Yes" to the import of American Hollywood films, and just five years later the first of them was shown throughout the territory of half-destroyed Yugoslavia. That was in 1953, and the film was *Dangerous When Wet* staring Esther Williams. This was the time of the cheerful socialist body culture, "body-pictures" (images and messages written on stadium grass by the bodies of Yugoslav youth), collective strengthening of the muscles, and unshakeable faith in a better future. Esther Williams, as a Hollywood version of this, easily won the hearts of the Yugoslav audience.

Only two men in my life had dimples on their chins: my grandfather and Kirk Douglas.

"Look," my mother used to say, pointing at a photograph of my grandfather, "Grandad has a dimple on his chin. Like Kirk Douglas."

My mother was a passionate movie fan and thanks to her passion I was introduced at a tender age to the uncomfortable wooden benches of the provincial movie theater.

The first chewing gum to appear on the Yugoslav market was exciting not because of the newly discovered art of chewing but because of the little pictures of Hollywood actors in which the gum was wrapped. In my postwar childhood, deprived of toys, those pictures were real riches, perhaps because they were our only riches. We collected the pictures, exchanged them, and stuck them into albums. I believe that we outdid the film critics of the time in our knowledge of the names of Hollywood actors.

It was only later, when the children of my generation grew up, that other pictures appeared: soccer players, cartoon characters, pop stars. And other things too: real toys, real picture books, and television. In a word, I knew what Kirk Douglas looked like before I knew what a real little girl's doll looked like.

I no longer remember how, but in that Hollywood childhood my generation knew the addresses of Hollywood stars. The most willing correspondent was Tony Curtis. Many of us received a signed photograph from him. But I had in my possession something that no one else had: a letter from Kirk Douglas and his signed photograph. It was all real, the letter in the unknown English language and the signature.

I never found out what Kirk Douglas wrote to me in the letter. I lost it before I could read it.

Then I forgot about Kirk Douglas. Then several famous film stars came to our country; they mostly played Germans, and more rarely Parisians. The most famous of them all was Richard Burton, who played Tito in one Yugoslav film.

My Hollywood childhood passed like children's measles, without, it seems, leaving any trace. In the meantime I became a writer. And I wouldn't have much reason to remember Kirk Douglas today if I had not recently come across a magazine with a shiny cover. In it I read an interview with the now very, very old Hollywood actor.

I learned that Kirk Douglas had just finished his sixth book, entitled *Climbing Mountains: My Search for Meaning.* Explaining his title, the famous actor said: "I believe that our life is like constantly climbing a mountain." The elderly actor explained that six years earlier, having survived an accident in which he broke his spine, he had felt the need to write this book. "I usually write in the morning. I jot my ideas down on music paper. Then Urila, my assistant, types them into the computer, edits them, and then I read it all through again and I'm surprised: How magnificent . . . ," said Kirk Douglas.

As I read these lines, I was overcome by a sudden, vague sadness. I tried to recall the face of Kirk Douglas from the little chewing gum picture. I tried to restore that child's sense of fascination with distant worlds. I wanted to return for a moment to the time when actors were just actors, not writers. I wanted to go back to the time when I feverishly read the works of writers who were just writers, not actors. And then the sadness became an inner protest. The protest came from the sudden sense of my historical moment; the thought that everyone in the world has become a writer, literature was not a mountain peak which I had been trying to climb for years, driven by the romantic notion that it belonged only to the persistent and dedicated, and that it was therefore only literary mountain-climbers who earned the right to write.

And then the inner protest quite suddenly gave way to a sense of almost mystical oneness. Was it not magnificent, I wondered, to have come all the way from a provincial movie theater to the peak reserved for actors and writers—here I was, writing, like Kirk Douglas himself! And when these reflections about metaphorical mountain climbing began to make me dizzy, it occurred to me that I would never know what Kirk Douglas had written to me in that letter, which I had so stupidly lost. I felt a sudden urge to reply to him, to write something about the magnificence of this truly historic moment:

Dear Mr. Douglas, You don't know me, but I have known you for a long time. . . .

1997

Alchemy

This is not a battle to fight.—Graffiti in a New York restaurant

I read in the newspaper that at an auction at Sotheby's in London a small tin of shit sold for £17,250. I see that the word "small" slipped out as I wrote that, as though the news would be more acceptable if it had been a bigger tin of shit. In his day, the Italian artist Piero Manzoni produced ninety tins filled with shit. The tins were numbered and signed, and sold at the current price of gold. An acquaintance of mine, an art dealer, assures me that the price was laughably low.

"If I had a Manzoni tin I could get 150,000 bucks for it without even trying," he assured me.

It turns out that Manzoni's tins are very rare today. Maybe skeptical buyers opened them to check whether they really did contain shit.

"While the price of gold is more or less stable, the price of shit has seen astronomical growth in the last thirty years. And it's still rising," claimed my acquaintance.

The transmutation of shit into gold is nevertheless no simple thing, for if it were we would all be rich. You need institutions, galleries, media, a market, publicity, interpreters (those who will explain the meaning of the artistic gesture), promoters, art dealers, critics, and, of course, consumers. Even when the shit is well packaged there is no guarantee that the transmutation will succeed.

The greatest shock for an East European writer who turned up in the Western literary marketplace was provoked by the absence of aesthetic criteria.

Criteria of literary evaluation were the capital which our Easterner assiduously accumulated his whole literary life. And then it turned out that this capital wasn't worth shit.

In the non-commercial East European cultures, there were no divisions into good and bad literature. There was *literature* and there was *trash*. Culture was divided into official culture and underground culture. Underground literature, as a resistance movement, occupied far more space (justifiably or not) on the unofficial scale of literary values. East European writers moved in a world of clear aesthetic coordinates, at least that's what they believed. In their underground literary workshops, they diligently tempered the steel of their literary convictions. In return, they received abundant moral and emotional support from their readership. Both writers and their readers had endless amounts of time at their disposal, both everyday time and "historical" time. And for someone to have any idea at all of what is really good, he needs time.

When East European writers finally began crawling out of their underground, they stepped into the global literary marketplace like self-confident literary arbiters, as unfailing connoisseurs of difference. They brought with them an awareness of their chosen position in this world (the Muses decided, not them), and a conviction that they had an unalienable right to literary art.

Their encounter with the literary market was the biggest shock of their writing lives, a loss of the ground under their feet, a terrible blow to their writers' egos.

"Oh, you're a writer?"

"Yes," our Easterner replies, trying to sound like a modest and well-brought-up person who does not want to humiliate those who have not been chosen.

"What a coincidence! Our ten-year-old daughter is just finishing a novel. We even have a publisher!"

This is merely the first insult that our Easterner has to swallow. He himself does not have a publisher. And he will soon discover that the world of the literary marketplace is densely populated with the "chosen," with his fellow writers. His fellow writers are prostitutes who write their memoirs, sportsmen who describe their sporting lives, girlfriends of renowned murderers who describe the murderer from a more intimate perspective, housewives bored with daily life who have decided to try the creative life; there are lawyer-writers, fisherman-writers, literary critic-writers, innumerable searchers after their own identity, a whole army of those whom someone has offended, raped, or beaten up, or whose toes have been stepped on, and who rush to inform the world in writing of the drama of their long-repressed injury.

Our Easterner is profoundly shaken. He does not believe that all these "colleagues" have the same rights as he does, that in the world of literary democracy everyone is equal, that everyone has the right to a book and to literary success. He does not, however, abandon the hope that (literary-historical) justice will prevail in the end, that the very next day everything will resume its place, that housewife-writers will stay housewives and fisherman-writers fishermen. He has nothing against democracy itself. On the contrary, coming from where he has come from he is the first to recognize its value, but not in literature and art, for God's sake!

Our Easterner is mistaken. The highly exciting life of a fisherman has greater commercial value than an East European's thoughts about what good literature is supposed to be. And the world of the literary marketplace is not only a world of momentary glamour, as our Easterner believes by way of consolation. It is not writers, arbiters of taste, or critics, but the powerful literary marketplace that establishes aesthetic values.

Recently, during a short visit to Moscow, I met a writer. She looked most impressive, covered in sequins and feathers. If I had met her in New York I would have thought she was a transvestite. She gave me two volumes of her book *Notes on Bras (Zapiski na liftchikakh)*. The author was a so-called woman of the people, a former chambermaid or something. She had written a novel about her feminine communist experiences. And the book was selling like hotcakes, she said.

"And what has Solzhenitsyn been doing lately?" I asked stupidly. I really wasn't that interested in Solzhenitsyn at the time.

"Huh?" gawped the author of *Notes on Bras* blankly.

In the world of trash, wrote Vladimir Nabokov, it is not the book that brings success, but the reading public.

Recently, out of curiosity, I visited the website of the author of the iconic book *The Alchemist*. The work, which critics describe as interdenominational, transcendental, and inspirational, is a bag of wind with millions of readers throughout the world. Out of some two hundred enraptured readers on the web, only two expressed mild reservations about the alchemist's talent. The skeptics were immediately pounced upon by *The Alchemist's* devotees, who asked that Amazon.com deny web access to any such comments.

I wondered why the consumers of victorious products were so fierce and intolerant. I had encountered the same aggressive tone, the same readiness for a fight to the end, each time I had expressed doubt in the value of any work which has millions of devotees. What is it that unites the million-strong army of lovers of *The Alchemist* so firmly and so easily divides the small group of lovers of Bohumil Hrabal? What is it that drives millions of people to shed tears as they watch *Titanic,* and drives a lunatic to deface a well-known painting in a Dutch museum? What is it that drives millions of people all over the world to weep for Lady Di, but to be indifferent when their next-door neighbor dies? I think I know the answer, but I would prefer to keep quiet, for the answer makes me tremble with terror.

"I know perfectly well that the book is shit," said a friend of mine, a teacher of literature at a European university, about some book. "But I looooove it!" he howled, drawing out the "o."

"Americans love junk. It's not the junk that bothers me, it's the love," said George Santayana. He said it at a time when he did not yet know that we were all one day going to become Americans.

But still, there is, presumably, something in the very nature of shit that makes it so loooooved. And however much the theoreticians of popular culture try to explain why shit ought to be loved, the most attractive aspect of shit is nevertheless its availability. Shit is accessible to everyone, shit is what unites us, we can stumble across shit at every moment, step in it, slip on it, shit follows us wherever we go, shit waits patiently on our doorstep ("Like shit in the rain" goes one popular Yugoslav saying). So who wouldn't love it! And love alone is the magic formula that can transform shit into gold.

1999

Women, Smoking, and Literature

Consider this scene in *The Forty-First,* an old Soviet film based on the novel of the same name by Boris Lavrenev. The story is about a brave young Red Army soldier, a woman, who has captured an enemy, a handsome White Guard officer. The two of them spend some time in a deserted hut, waiting for her unit to arrive. The Red Army soldier, who has a warm and non-dogmatic heart, falls in love with her handsome ideological enemy. At one moment her prisoner runs out of cigarette paper. She magnanimously offers the prisoner her only precious possession, a modest notebook of her own poems. The White Guard officer wraps his tobacco in the Red Army soldier's poems and in full view of the entire film audience brazenly smokes, until he has smoked up her very last line.

Can we imagine the scene the other way round? No. For this scene, how-ever naive and touching, is far more than a film scene, it is the metaphorical synopsis of the history of women's writing, the relation of women to their own creativity and the relation of men towards women's creativity.

Throughout the history of women's writing, men have transformed women's literary passion into ashes. Throughout history women have sacri-ficed themselves for literature. Many literatures have survived dark times thanks exclusively to women. Let us recall the way Nadezhda Mandelstam resolutely memorized Osip's poems. That is how she saved his great poetry from Stalin's powerful finger on the delete key. Let us remember wives, lovers, female friends, female fans, translators, companions, benefactors, copyists, typists, proofreaders, devoted editors, wise women writers of literary introductions, agents, inspirers, muses, literary advisers, fierce supporters, tender fillers of literary pipes, painstaking cooks, hardworking archivists, librarians, passionate readers, reliable keepers of manuscripts, living sphinxes in posthumous literary shrines, diligent cleaners of writers' studies, those who keep away the dust from collected works and literary busts, frenetic enthusiasts of societies for the adoration of dead and living poets, women, women, women. . . .

Women have saved literary texts while men have destroyed them. How men—dictators, potentates, censors, lunatics, pyromaniacs, military commanders, emperors, leaders, policemen—have hated the written word! If a woman has occasionally wrapped fresh fish in the verse of a minor poet, what is that compared to the books burned under the rule of the Chinese emperor Shih Huang Ti? If women sometimes used an epic poem to wrap a cake in the oven to keep it from burning, what is that in comparison to the tons of manuscripts destroyed by the KGB? If a woman used a little book to light a fire in the family hearth, what is that to the smoke of the volumes which burned on Nazi pyres? If some woman used the page of a novel to clean the windows, what is that compared to the ash left after Karadžić and Mladić's shelling of the Sarajevo National Library?

Can we imagine the reverse image? No. It is simply unthinkable. In history, women were readers, women were those little flies caught on the hook of the written word, women were the reading public. Thus, in one little literature, Croatian, in the middle of the nineteenth century, male writers had to persuade women readers to stop reading literature in German because there was simply no one to read them, the local writers. "The patriotic heart breaks with sorrow, on hearing that not only the high-born, but even the simple burghers' daughters speak disparagingly of our national tongue," complains a nineteenth-century Croatian writer. And Croatian readers, kind-hearted women, took pity on them and began, yawning with boredom, to read local writers. The literature of that small country began with them, with women readers.

Women were always the house spirits of literature. Metaphorically speaking, into every literary house is built the shadow of its real builder, a woman, some Mary, some Jane, some Vera. . . . Stacy Schiff, the author of the biography *Vera (Mrs. Vladimir Nabokov)* writes: "From the list of things Nabokov bragged about never having learned to do—type, drive, speak German, retrieve a lost object, fold an umbrella, answer the phone, cut a book's pages, give the time of day to a philistine—it is easy to deduce what Vera spent her life doing."

Let us go back to the beginning and say that the histories of women, literature, and smoke are inseparable; it is virtually a shared history. It is only women and books which were burned on the Inquisition's pyres. The role of men in historical ash is statistically negligible. In the history of mankind, whenever required, women-witches (literate women) and books (the source of knowledge and pleasure) have been proclaimed the work of the Devil.[1]

Let us interrupt our sorrowful tale here with a brighter example, Russian once again. A Moscow mother was very worried about her son, although there was no reason for it: her son was an excellent pupil, a lover of literature, devoted to Pushkin. But still, this mother was terrified of the greatest evil, drugs, so she regularly went through her son's pockets. One day, she finally found what she was looking for: a little, dark brown lump carefully wrapped in foil. Instead of destroying the fateful lump, this courageous woman decided to try the power of the drug on herself. Although she had no experience whatsoever, she somehow managed to roll a joint and light it. Her general sense of well-being and relaxation was rudely interrupted by her son who appeared in the doorway.

"Where's my little packet?" he shouted.

"I smoked it," said his mother cheerfully.

The little lump was not pot, as the mother had thought, but earth from

---

[1] In Taylor Hackford's American film *Devil's Advocate,* there is an interesting modern representation of the Devil. The Devil (Al Pacino) and his female crew can be identified by two details: they smoke (no one smokes in America today apart from dark forces!) and they use foreign languages eloquently (the educated are also among the dark forces).

the grave of Pushkin, her son's relic. So the mother smoked Pushkin. And so this courageous woman, without knowing it, avenged the selfless Red Army soldier's verse which had been turned into ash. This anonymous woman, without knowing it, perhaps turned a new, revolutionary page in the history of literature. I say, "perhaps." In any case: I thank her!

1997

Optimism Strengthens the Organism

The fall of communism brought about something that happens in nature whenever the biological balance is upset. Many things disappeared from the contemporary cultural environment, including ideological labels. No one nowadays would proclaim in public that someone is a *communist* or even a *capitalist*. The old rhetoric—*neo-communists, Marxists, anti-capitalists*—only escapes from the lips of the occasional CNN reporter who has forgotten how things are. The words have disappeared because the ideological context in which they had meaning has also disappeared. The vacuum has been filled by money, which appears to have become the only ideology.

Romantics—people who still believe that ideologies motivate people, and that the main cause of nationalism in former Yugoslavia lies in communism, which brutally suppressed the right to ethnic identities—should look at the property holdings of today's nationalists in power. Even a cursory glance will show that nationalism, and the accompanying war, was simply an ideological-advertising jingle, a stimulus for the crude acquisition of capital whose dimensions ranged from a stolen video recorder to stolen factories, according to one's means and abilities. Let us not forget that even Andrei Chikatilo—the cannibal from Rostov who ate fifty of his comrades—tried during his trial to justify his unusual appetite by communist repression. Anyone who still believes that religious ideology was crudely shackled during communist times should visit "liberated" Croatia: in every village, like kernels of corn in popcorn machines, Virgins leap out, appearing to children in open fields or to housewives in the form of mist through cottage windows, while the locals in their liberated religious fervor rub their hands in glee. More Virgins mean more tourists!

Money, therefore, and not convictions. But it turns out that life without ideology is as empty as an unfurnished house. A person feels uncomfortable in such a space, unaccustomed to it. That is why the emptied space has been swiftly occupied by new, apparently innocent ideological flora: *optimism*. Former communists, modern capitalists, nationalists, religious fanatics, they have all become optimists. Optimists are winners. Why? Because their ideology is natural and agreeable, everyone can agree with them. Why does everyone agree with them? Because people like optimists, and pessimists are bores, always spoiling your good mood.

For instance, two of my fellow countrymen were young doctors interning at a hospital in the American town where they lived. Both of them worked hard at the hospital, hoping to get permanent jobs there. At work, the first one used to answer every "How are you today?" with "Great!" The second, who had brought habits with him from his former homeland, said "So-so, could be better." The first one got a job, the other did not. When I heard this, I agreed with the hospital's decision, and I still do. There is nothing more depressing than a depressed doctor.

Optimism as a mental commitment has permeated all human activities, including the sphere of so-called freedom of thought. As with the doctors, I would be in complete agreement here too, except that optimism has a stain on its ideological record: the slogan about the individual commitment to optimism comes from the Stalinist armory. If anything has survived Stalinism itself, it is the Stalinist demand for optimism. Let us recall that seventy years ago, in the Soviet Union, *defeatists* paid for the sin of defeatism with their lives. Accusing someone of *spreading defeatism* condemned him to several years in Stalinist camps. A *defeatist* was the devil incarnate: a national traitor, an enemy of the people, an underhanded skeptic, a provocateur, an anticommunist, in short a skunk in human form. Eeyore, the melancholic donkey, is nothing other than a *defeatist* in the Stalinist meaning of the word. If there had been camps for literary characters back then, Eeyore would have been among the first inmates.

Be that as it may, the world in recent times has been divided into optimists and pessimists. We are living in a state of cultural war. The optimists are the "good guys," the peace-loving majority, while the pessimists are the "bad guys," a minority that exists only in order to spoil things for the majority.

Who are the culture-optimists? They are populists; defenders of marketing modernity; lovers of various media, styles, and genres; denigrators of elitist culture, hierarchy, and class; admirers of techno-culture and all that it entails; fans of speed, globalism, and every piece of fashionable cultural junk. Versace and Virgil, Naomi Campbell and Virginia Woolf, Michael Jackson and James Joyce, Madonna and Mickey Mouse, Xena and Sappho, rap and pop, Dr. Atkins and Martin Amis, the renowned and the marginalized, white and black, Tom Clancy and Paul Virilio—they all mingle promiscuously in cultural mega-space. Mega-promiscuity is modernity.

It is true that the culture-optimist is not particularly consistent, but why should he be? When he chooses wine, for example, the optimist will consult a wine expert, because only an expert knows how to differentiate between tastes and aromas, sharpness and sweetness, kinds of grapes and the side of the valley where they have grown. The optimist will admit that he is lost without such an arbiter. The fact that he publicly defends cultural populism does not mean that he himself has to drink Budweiser. Given a choice between Varteks (a former Yugoslav brand of clothing) and Versace, he will of course choose Versace. However, when it's a matter of literature, the culture-optimist will immediately take the side of Danielle Steel and agree with the people who are indifferent to Dante, because Dante "doesn't relate to them." Whereas Danielle "does." In literature and art, the culture-optimist will furiously attack any attempt at arbitration. Why? Because it is precisely this, value judgment, that his enemy the culture-pessimist advocates.

What are the culture-pessimists like? Complaining, apocalyptic, tedious, nostalgic, elitist, conservative, dogmatic, boring, defenders of traditional values, "professors," devoted worshippers of the Western Canon, polishers of busts in museums, gravediggers, takers of the pulse of dying art, adorers of

Adorno, moralists, "dead white males." It is a bit confusing that this "dead white male," this "zombie," is treated as a serious danger, and that we should be living in a state of perpetual cultural war on account of a corpse.

As far as I am concerned, I have chosen the right side in this war. I am an optimist—converted, I admit, but converts are the most zealous. Having chosen my side, I have decided to reactivate the rusty weapons of communist cultural ideology (I do know something about this, and in war every bit of knowledge is welcome) in the fight against our enemies, the White Male Corpse.

In early communist Yugoslavia, there was a practice of linking Culture and Labor, which meant workers. Unfortunately, I did not personally experience that practice, but I do know that metalworkers received free tickets to *Swan Lake,* that miners went on collective outings to museums of modern art, that opera singers gave concerts in steelworks and coal mines. Once, in communist times, I was at the Bolshoi Theater in Moscow, part of an audience that consisted almost entirely of miners. Although it turned out later that they were actually tourists, drunken Finns, who only looked like miners.

In this early phase of communism, Culture was not allowed to be elite, nor was Labor allowed to be impolite and refuse the anti-elite hand which Culture so cordially proffered.

As an optimist and a writer I have decided to repair the broken relationship between Culture and Labor. I sent a letter to Gucci, in which I suggest that for an agreed consideration I shall dress the characters of my next novel in Gucci outfits. I also wrote to Miele, the Mercedes of household appliances, and offered them the exclusive rights to have the heroine of my next novel clean her apartment with a Miele vacuum cleaner. I sent two letters simultaneously, one to Philip Morris and the other to Marina Rinaldi, the fashion designer for plus-sized women, with my proposal for a novel called *Big Woman Meets Marlboro Man.* I sent a similar letter to the Amsterdam diamond cutters, because diamond cutters are a kind of miner, after all, and if money is hard to come by there is nothing wrong with diamonds. I fully expect to get their answers soon—all positive, no doubt.

From the heights, our new gods, the Planners, smile down on me. Who are the Planners? The Planners are manipulators, advertising experts, who reflect about Nike sneakers as though it were a matter of Shakespeare, so that their customers, when they buy Nikes, can feel that at the same time they have instantly mastered the whole of Shakespeare. Incidentally, Planners do not like pessimists. We, the optimists, are God's chosen ones. Why? Because only we, the optimists, are reliable consumers.

2000

4   Country Cousin

"Who lives there?"

"I do. At least I thought I did. But I suppose I don't. After all, we can't all have houses."

A Little Red Dot

A visit to the Slavic Department library of a European university is an experience of a special kind, like a visit to a planetarium where the sensitive visitor confronts his real place in the universe. The visit is upsetting, particularly if our visitor comes from the former Yugoslavia, and is a creative writer and a book lover. The full confrontation with a shelf of books deprives our visitor of his last illusions.

For the visitor knows every book: its author, the milieu in which it was forged, its biography. Now, in a neglected corner of some Slavic library, he has the chance to see its end, its last resting place among books which are rarely if ever checked out.

The visitor will find Serbian, Croatian, Bosnian, Slovenian, and Macedonian books on the shelf, all here, all equally alone in an enforced library community. Andrić and Aralica, the alphabet is as merciless as the sword of justice, there is no right of appeal. Kiš and Koš are pressed together like Siamese twins.

The visitor is at first demoralized by the poverty of the collection, but he accepts the selection resignedly, as the decision of some higher literary court. The visitor notices the traces of the bureaucratic hand of the librarian, but also traces of the capricious and exclusive hands of visiting lecturers in Croatian or Serbian literature. Some visiting lecturer has made sure that the library is abundantly supplied with his own books, or those of his friends, another has provided it with the books of his fellow tribesmen, a third, a local patriot, with books from his region. The visitor notices titles and authors he has never heard of: nobodies are often the most aggressive, they have to take care of themselves. Standing like that in the dusty corner of the Slavic library, the visitor reads the bookshelf as his own destiny—reads it by touch, like a fortune-teller.

He is suddenly overwhelmed by a powerful sense of self-pity. He wonders whether it was worth the effort: his lengthy schooling, his cultural memory packed with names, quotations and facts which he will never be able to share with anyone, other than members of his own tribe and the occasional rare foreign (Yugo)slavist. He wonders whether there was any point wasting years of his life to end up on a small, dusty bookshelf.

The visitor stands before the shelf, as though rooted to the spot, without any desire to take a single one of the books in his hand. But on the spine of one of the books he notices a little red dot. Encouraged by the dot, for some reason, he takes the book off the shelf and hurries to find the librarian. The librarian is an aging woman, with a pale, lined face, yet another human instance of merging over time with one's surroundings.

"What does this little red dot mean?"

"That the book may not be taken out of the library."

"Why? It's quite new."

"Because those are the books that are usually not returned."

"You mean people steal them?"

"Yes."

Our visitor hurries back and looks around for red dots.

The visitor stares at that dot and his sudden cheerfulness is replaced by a feeling of bitterness. He knows full well all the battles that the little book had to wage in order in the end to earn peace, a miniature honor, a small mark of difference, a victorious red dot.

First of all, it had to survive a provincial literary milieu. And the local milieu, as it now is, resembles a lengthy and tortuous passage through a tunnel, through "a hot rabbit."[1] Yes, even in the remote Southern European

---

[1] "The hot rabbit" was a cruel method of torturing prisoners in Goli Otok, the former Yugoslav camp for political detainees. The newly arrived prisoner had to undergo an "initiation": passing through rows of prisoners who spat at him, beat him ferociously, or stoned him.

literary provinces one lives a life which is often fiercer, more dangerous, and more difficult than life in a literary metropolis. The Serbian, Croatian, Bosnian, Montenegrin literary provincial setting, seen from the outside, reminds one of a nest of dedicated destroyers of books: the paper bacteria which work away assiduously at literature. No one survives alone over there, you survive in herds, flocks, packs. Literary species always move in formation, like dolphins. Together, coupled to one another, they form a garland, a swastika, a red star, according to the needs of the historical moment and the desire of the current master. They live on one another, they survive only in symbiosis. Not one of them nourishes a great talent; they feed on each other's. They live in *sties,* their rewards from the previous régime, and now they spit on that régime without, however, giving up their sties. After all, they waged all their battles for sties: an editorship, a literary prize, an important position. That was the peak, there was no higher they could go. They all gave somebody something in order to get something themselves, they all denied someone something for they had been denied themselves. They hate each other, scheme against one another, shed each other's blood, bare their teeth, bite, growl, bark, cluck, hiss, but they stay together, for they need each other, they can only survive together. They publish their books, big and small, and jostle on the shelves of their national literatures; there is no place for them, it seems, on any other shelf. They are isolated, and proud of it, only the isolated can occupy themselves uninterruptedly with their own activities. They show an enviable vitality, they hang on with parasitic tenacity. No storm has yet been able to move them. They are tough, swollen with blood, they don't miss a chance to sting each other. They possess an enviable elasticity, they can transform themselves in a moment, survival is more important to them than life. In the name of survival, they lower their moral standards, lie, mimic one another, mutate, disguise themselves. They are by nature denunciators and servants. They gladly pronounce big words, they concern themselves with "national affairs," culture, literature, art. Their intellectual activities are reduced to judgment: we'll throw this out, cut that, destroy this one, eliminate that one. They multiply, they accept the weak into their ranks just so that they themselves will appear stronger. They are greedy, they never have enough.

Recently they pointed their heavy guns at one another, went to war in their one and only language and divided it into three—Croatian, Serbian, and Bosnian, although they are the only ones to see any difference. The well-meaning foreign Slavist hears all those languages as dialects with insignificant distinctions, but what do foreigners know, and it's none of their business anyway! Then they dug trenches between their local literatures, and divided them into three as well—Croatian, Serbian, and Bosnian— they erected frontiers, they established literary checkpoints, they introduced literary passports, threw "aliens" out of the libraries, cleansed the school curricula, and now, thank goodness, there are no longer any "aliens" among them. Even that was not enough for them: they shelled libraries, destroyed thousands of books, each according to his abilities, all in the name of their identity, their language, their thousand-year literacy. And that was not enough. They erased their own writers from their culture, those individuals who did not suit the new times, those who "strutted self-importantly." They made illiterates into ministers of culture, editors, publishers, members of the academy. What's more, they appointed as librarians people whose job description included throwing "inappropriate" books into the garbage. There are too many books anyway, *books only gather dust.* But actually, there are more books now than before. They publish books by their presidents— Croatian, Serbian, and Bosnian—by the presidents' wives, generals, politicians, soldiers, and murderers. They are zealots, they are ardent, they lobby, they write protest letters, they agitate, they demand that there should be departments of their languages and literatures at foreign universities, they demand their own, exclusive national shelves in foreign libraries, they impose themselves, carry out wars in cyberspace, angrily refuse to be with one another. (Us with those foreigners? For God's sake, it would be like shoving Goethe and Musil onto the same shelf!) They defend their national culture, their national identity. They are active, they never have enough activity, they denounce their own writers as traitors, are consumed with jealousy if one of those *traitors* succeeds in publishing a book *abroad,* they write venomous anonymous letters to foreign newspapers, they protest against their *countrymen,* those renegades, they will pursue them to Alaska if necessary, those people must be stopped.... They rarely buy books, because they rarely read, because who has room for all those books in their house, *books only gather dust.* They are active, they never have enough activity, they leave important monuments behind them: the Croats left behind the Mostar Bridge at the bottom of the Neretva River, the Serbs transformed the Sarajevo National Library into a ton of carbon. Ruins are their mark, their icon, their signature, their cultural monument, symbol, and metaphor—ruins are the real result of their literary efforts.

Standing in the dark of the empty Slavic library, staring at the little red dot on the spine of a book, the visitor relives the dramatic history of the books written in the small Yugo-languages, a history which no one can transmit to anyone else, because no one would be in a position to understand it, because it is hard to understand. The visitor knows that that little red dot on the spine of the book is the greatest literary prize that it is possible for a writer from the Yugoslav literary provinces to achieve, more significant than a Nobel Prize. It is the result of a secret ballot, in which anonymous visitors to the library—Croatian, Serbian, and Bosnian—have chosen the only cultural heritage that they recognize as alive and meaningful. Who knows who these visitors were, students, refugees, exiles, lovers and thieves of books, losers who have chosen their literary king? And who actually cares? They have made their choice, and the other books lie in the dust, now and forever.

The red dot pulsates in the empty corner of the Slavic library. Our visitor stands rooted to the spot and stares. Then he carefully takes the red-dotted book off the shelf and tenderly puts it into his pocket, as though it were a living creature, a lost mouse. And leaves the library with a bitter smile on his lips.

1998

How I Could Have Been
Ivana Trump and Where I Went Wrong

What is the point of newborn states?

What is the point of newborn states, which, as their poetically disposed rulers like to say, *must be born in blood?* What is the point of those babies who try, with their tedious bawling, to make themselves heard over the noise of the world?

I possess the passport of one such country, Croatia. The fact that I have a passport does not make me competent to judge matters of state, still, I dare to say something, and my competence, as I only recently discovered, emerges from the statistical nature of things.

A Chinese person recently asked me, "All right, so how many of you Croats are there?"

"About four and a half million."

"Oh, that's great, you all must know each other!"

Small states are easier to grasp than large ones.

Small newborn states like Croatia offer their inhabitants a unique lesson in nature and society, history, anthropology, sociology, and the psychology of human behavior. Such an opportunity comes no more than once in a lifetime, and the inhabitants of stable states do not get it even once. In addition, newborn states are more exciting than stable ones, for just as newborn babies change their parents' lives, newborn states fundamentally alter their citizens' lives. That is what happened to me, which is perhaps why I judge matters of state with such self-confidence.

Newborn states launder both dirty money and dirty secrets. The quickest and most efficient way for a criminal to become a hero, or for a poor fool to become a rich man, is to fight for the birth of a little state, because there is the ideal place for creative financial transactions, the rapid and efficient acquisition of wealth and power, and that villa you've always wanted, especially if it belongs to someone else. These countries are breeding grounds for new and miraculous forms of human behavior. As if under a microscope, you can see patterns of life so vigorous, shameless, and unambiguous, that the anthropological agitation quite takes your breath away.

The circulation of human material in the newborn states is astonishing: some pour out from inside, others pour in from outside. Changes of position are carried out with the speed of accelerated film. Return to a homeland which is about to be born and help the state midwives: there is no better time to move from the position of a Croatian emigré working in a Canadian pizzeria to the position of Minister of Defense, or from being a village primary-school teacher to being Minister of Culture and Education. There is no quicker way to move from being an illiterate plumber to being Minister of Foreign Affairs than wholeheartedly congratulating the little state on its birth. There is no easier way to come by a consular post in India, Australia, or America than to write a poem in praise of the newborn baby. There is no easier way to become a state sculptor, painter, theater director, writer than to hold the baby's bottle and wipe its ass at the right moment.

In short, the time of the birth of a new state is unusually attractive: it dynamizes human relations, galvanizes its citizens until they're dizzy, makes what was impossible up until then possible. The reverse as well: there is no quicker and more efficient way to be left without anything and to find yourself with one suitcase in some foreign country than by publicly saying that you find the business of birth nauseating, especially when it's bloody. That is what happened to me. And thank goodness I had a suitcase.

Who is Ivana Trump?

Ivana Trump was born in Czechoslovakia in 1949 and grew up in the small town of Gottwaldov. Her father was in the furniture business and a former champion swimmer. As a little girl, Ivana used to spend summer vacations with her parents on the Adriatic coast. She loved the Adriatic, like all Czechs, but her first unhappy memories date from there as well. The local people in those pretourist days could be very unkind to those who were insolvent in hard currency, the *Dumplings,* and very kind to those who were solvent in hard currency, the *Krauts.* Ivana stopped training as a swimmer, perhaps because of this Adriatic trauma, and took up skiing. She became a member of the Czech team and a beauty. As a beauty, she appeared on the cover of the Czech fashion magazine *Moda.* In 1973, she emigrated to Canada, to be with her boyfriend, the skier George Syrovatka. The boyfriend had a sports equipment store. Ivana became a model. Just three years later, she traded up her brief career as a model and George's wife for the career of being Donald Trump's. Anyone who does not know who Donald Trump is should go to New York and visit the Trump Tower on Fifth Avenue, not far from the Plaza Hotel. In the glorious decade of her married career, Ivana Trump rose to be manager of the above-mentioned Plaza, and after her divorce in 1990, she got both the Plaza and lavish severance pay, and became a success-ful businesswoman, writer, and active participant in the international jet set. "I am not an actress. I can't dance or sing. I am not a superstar. I am a per-sonality. I travel extensively, and wherever I go the perception of me helps me to sell my products. Maybe I'm selling me," she once said.

What have I got to do with Ivana Trump?

Nothing. But if you insist:

a) I was in the Plaza once. Someone took me there for tea with English tea cakes.

b) I was reading the *New York Times Book Review* once, and came across a lengthy review of Ivana Trump's novel. I wouldn't have noticed it if

Joseph Brodsky hadn't received in the very same issue an unjustly malicious review of his latest book *Watermark*. One reviewer vilified Brodsky for his language "jammed with metaphors," and the other praised Ivana for her analytical intelligence, especially in the parts of her book about Czech communism before the Russian occupation. I did not read Ivana Trump's novel, but I saw a TV movie based on it. I liked the scene of Ivana's spectacular escape over the Czech border the best. She was so fit, she flew over the border on skis. And that is how she made it to Canada, all on skis.

c) Once, when I was in New York, I came across a Czech writer who told me how she had been to visit Ivana Trump, trying to persuade her to give money for the impoverished Czech library collections. Ivana Trump gave nothing.

d) In London once, I found myself at a party where I was out of place. Ivana Trump was there as well. My host introduced me to her condescendingly, as though he were introducing me to Thomas Mann himself. I offered her my hand and said: "Pleased to meet you." She said nothing. I found her appearance somehow touching. With her exaggeratedly bleached hair, too-heavy make-up, and lips like fresh hot dogs she reminded me for a moment of the heroines of those wonderful Czech films of the seventies.

What has Ivana Trump got to do with me, and what has the state got to do with it all?

In André Gide's little book *Marshlands,* which I have always read as an apology for losers, there is a sentence which runs: "Victorious military leaders have a strong odor." This quote got stored permanently in my brain.

I left my newborn statelet in order to get away from war profiteers, the real victors of the war in former Yugoslavia: the types with oiled hair, gold chains around their necks and Rolex watches on their wrists, newly acquired toys (weapons, factories, yachts, and hotels). I ran away from the illiterates who had cheerfully occupied posts designed for the literates: faculties, schools,

publishing houses, newspapers. I ran away from the victors who had con-
quered every inch of their new statelet with greasy cordiality and the oper-
etta din of their patriotism. I could not stand the smell of their victory.

Ivana Trump, on the other hand, ran straight to Croatia, to the same sea
she remembered from her childhood. From the local types with oiled hair
they say she bought toys: hotels, casinos, department stores. She promised to
help the natives, especially the female natives. *Croatian women are talented in
many ways, they cook well, they sew nicely, they are good painters,* she announced.
And for herself, for Ivana Trump the writer, she bought a trifle: the Split
daily newspaper *Free Dalmatia.* She would not get involved in editorial policy,
she said, she would just take a column that she would write herself.

What did the writer actually intend to say?

Whether Ivana Trump really bought the newspaper, as the Croatian media
maintained, I do not know, and it doesn't matter. But when my students
ask me how one becomes a writer, I reply with complete authority: "Take
up a sport and train like hell. Anything else could lead you in the wrong
direction."

And really, having become a writer of world renown, it would have been
difficult for Joseph Brodsky to become a brilliant skier, while it was easy for
Ivana Trump to go from being a skier to a writer, even a brilliant analyst of
political conditions in her former communist homeland, as the reviewer in
the *New York Times Book Review* said. Having myself become a writer, I
have little prospect of ever becoming a soccer player, but every soccer player
can easily occupy my territory: literature. Thus the well-known soccer player,
Davor Šuker, announced after the 1998 World Cup, where the Croatian
team won third place: *No offence to Croatian writers, but we have probably
just written the greatest fairy tale in the history of Croatian literature.*

1998

GW, the Gloomy Writer

"Have you all got something?" asked Christopher Robin with his mouth full.
"All except me," said Eeyore. "As usual."

In the brightly colored and noisy life of the literary marketplace there is one gloomy participant. He strolls into the marketplace for the first time in the style of Peter Sellers in the Blake Edwards movie *The Party,* like a man who has come to a place where he always belonged, only he had never been invited before. Nevertheless, bit by bit our participant loses his self-confidence. No one notices him in the general brilliance as he stands crestfallen near a distant, unobtrusive stall. There he spends less and less time doing what he came for—selling his literary produce—and more time grumbling. Grumbling is his favorite intellectual activity; he is an absolute champion grumbler. He comes from a culture of grumbling, grew up and was educated among people who had spent centuries grumbling. Just as every Norwegian puts on skis the moment he is born, just as everyone in Holland rides a bicycle, so our gloomy participant really has no equal in grumbling, especially because he is a writer, the mouthpiece of his grumbling nation.

We'll call our participant GW. His house has been blown down, the wall and the iron curtain do not protect him anymore, he has a historical copyright on misery, he deserves to be described.

GW reminds you of a pathetic figure from the literary provinces. When you notice him—you who are in the center or at least think you are—you are immediately filled with a sense of vague guilt. And here begins the story of seduction. Our literary type has an inferiority complex. People with complexes often become oppressors. So watch out, you who have nothing even though you are successful and in the center, you can easily be hooked.

How shall we, in our world of images, copies, mimicry, and virtuality, most easily recognize GW? By the fact that he never misses an opportunity for disparaging his fellow writers. The anecdote about Pasternak being summoned by Stalin and asked whether he thought Mandelstam was a good poet is the most accurate profile of the type. It isn't even necessary to tell the anecdote to the end; everyone knows what happened to Mandelstam.

Of course GW is cunning. To start with he pretends a bit, that he doesn't know X's work all that well, as a rule he doesn't read his fellow countrymen. But if you press him a little harder, he'll open his oppressed heart to you, spreading black ink around him like a cuttlefish, and you will see that GW knows his rival's works in detail.

GW is of course on intimate terms with writers such as Shakespeare, Goethe, Tolstoy; he talks about them as though he were a close member of their families. Perhaps it is because of this intimate relationship towards literary history that our GW finds it so easy to wave his bilious critical scissors about. When he has cut them all down, chopped them up, razed them to the ground, he feels calmer.

GW is most cutting about his contemporaries, those who write in his own little, unimportant language: if he is Bulgarian, he attacks Bulgarians; if he is Romanian, he attacks Romanians; if he is a Croat, he attacks Serbs; if he is a Serb, he attacks Croats. He will never miss a chance to say of his compatriots who have been translated into some more significant language that they are far, far better in translation. *If you only knew what those illiterates sound like in the original!*

GW is somewhat gentler with his famous foreign contemporaries. Thus he says authoritatively of Salman Rushdie that his success was due to political scandal, of Umberto Eco that he uses a teacher's tricks, of John Updike that he is a third-rate scribbler.

It turns out that GW is most pained by what is furthest from him, the Nobel Prize for instance. He is so vitriolic about every winner that anyone listening to his tirade will wonder for a moment whether it should not actually have been GW who received it. At the same time, GW uses his tirades to draw attention to his own high moral virtues, and these, of course, are the hardest to verify.

Unlike what he writes, GW's character is not that easy to read. First he plays the provincial game: he's a small writer from a small country, from a small literature, no one knows his language, he lives on the cultural periphery. If he is Russian, aware that he belongs to a major literature, he prefers to play the card of the historically traumatized writer. GW will so skillfully act confused that you won't notice you are showing him the way to the restaurant toilet because he can't even read the signs on the doors, poor thing.

Incidentally, now that we are in the restaurant where you are having lunch with GW, you should know that he won't even reach for his wallet. You will pay for the lunch, which is what you expected in any case, didn't you? GW feels that he has been personally, collectively, and historically mistreated and that is why he so naturally allows others to compensate him. Then, in the course of a stroll after lunch, he will gaze so blatantly at the shop windows, grumbling that he has to buy presents for his sizeable family, that you will immediately offer to help him. You will notice that GW never buys junk. Awkward, provincial, and modest as he is, he will buy himself shoes of a kind you perhaps could treat yourself to, but never would.

I once watched a compatriot of mine in Rome, who had bought himself a pair of Louis Vuitton shoes. Touched by my compatriot's awkwardness—and by both his historical and his recent trauma—his Italian translator bent down to tie his shoelaces for him. With elegant naturalness, GW permitted it.

GW never misses an opportunity to thrust his manuscripts and his press clippings into your hands. You won't know how it came about, but you will find yourself writing down the addresses of publishers and agents, warmly offering to write reader's reports. And GW, weighed down by a noble weariness, will complain that his own colleagues keep bombarding him with their talentless manuscripts, keep asking things of him, so that these half-literate nonentities with literary pretensions hardly leave him time for his own work.

GW appears exclusively in the male gender. That is why he experiences literature as an exclusively male thing. He gladly dedicates his books and poems to other male writers. To judge by the dedications, the literatures of the East European provinces have a deeply homosexual character. In literary discussions, he turns exclusively to men, he carries on polemics with men, he chooses literary examples only from among men, he forms eternal friendships only with men, he prides himself on his important, always male, acquaintances.

He tolerates his female colleagues, but doesn't take them seriously. If they are young, he flirts with them; he likes raising a toast to female beauty, motherhood, and female wisdom; if they are older (which means about his own age) he doesn't notice them. Privately he likes talking about women. His amorous-matrimonial biography is usually very rich. Women in the East European provinces wash writers' socks, copy their works, bring up their numerous children, fight for better fees for them, set terms with translators, learn foreign languages so as to be of service when GW is talking to foreign journalists. The geniuses they nurture don't get involved in such wearisome affairs. Afraid of his own extinction, GW likes to create warm, harem-like structures. He hopes (quite justifiably) that his surviving wives will maintain the eternal flame in his literary temple and take care of new editions (presumably that's why he keeps marrying ever-younger women). GW doesn't like cleaning out his writer's pigsty; he unconsciously leaves large quantities of evidence around, including ordinary bus tickets, in the hope that one day such things will find their place in a future literary museum in his name.

GW never learned to be a loner or an individualist, because he has never tried. Surrounded by harems in his private life, pampered by cliques, literary friendships, political groupings, editorial boards and similar structures in his public life, GW finds it hard to survive without his surroundings. That is why GW likes to use phrases such as *our literature, our generation.* GW always hides behind his group, his nation, his generation, his people, some literary trend, because without all that he feels exposed and naked, dependent only upon his own talent. And experience shows that no one has ever survived on his own talent.

Let us add here that GW's grumbling shouldn't be taken too seriously. In the culture he comes from, grumbling is often a form of socializing. When he opens his mouth to moan, you should immediately start complaining yourself. That's the best way to get rid of him. Because GW needs an audience, his favorite narrative strategy is the monologue.

Some twenty years ago, I met a young Croatian doctor who had written a novel to amuse himself. A perfectly decent "hospital novel." Many years later, he called me. He had managed to place his novel with an important New York publisher.

"Congratulations! Isn't that great!" I said.

"Like hell it is!" he grumbled angrily.

"It's a great thing to have a publisher like that take your book."

"I might as well never have published it! I've been surfing the Internet for several months now and there's not a word about me anywhere. What can I do?" my compatriot asked, in a despairing tone.

"I don't know, really. . . ."

"Do you think I'm being deliberately ignored because I'm a Croat?"

"It's hard to say. . . ."

"Then why don't they write about me?"

"Probably because they publish hundreds of novels like that every year. . . ."

"But my novel has already been named a best-seller in three countries!"

"Which three?"

"Croatia, Slovenia, and Slovakia!"

Today GW is an equal participant in the brightly colored and noisy life of the global literary market. For now he is selling what he has, his East European literary souvenirs. However, everything has its price on the literary marketplace, everything sells just as long as there are people to buy. That's why you should greet him, wave to him, notice him, smile at him, you ought to feel a little bit sorry for him, even if he is a killjoy and a party pooper. After all, his house has been blown down, and that's no laughing matter. That's why you should help him set up his stall. That's why you should wish him a nice, successful day.

1997

The Magnificent Buli

In small nations, the nest of the genius is hidden.—Petar Njegoš

In the typology of literary producers who have crawled out of closed, non-commercial cultures into the global literary market, there is one rare but interesting literary type. Let us say at once, the Magnificent Buli is a genius. Geniuses too are members of the literary family, not just the bearers of average talent who far outnumber them.

The first thing that differentiates Buli from his gloomy and grumbling East European fellow writers is his cheerfulness and friendliness. For example, he will cordially ask the first Italian he happens upon:

"So, how is Umbi these days, has he written anything new?"

"Umbi?" the puzzled Italian asks.

"Why, Umberto Eco!"

This innocent intimacy is the first symptom which can lead the investigator straight to the heart of Buli's psyche.

At the very center of Buli's genius is an eternally preserved image which is erased from most people's memory. We all recognize the image: a mother joyfully lifts up her baby, brings its little bottom wrapped in its diaper to her nose, sniffs gaily, scowls jokingly, *oof-oof, ugh-ugh,* she gurgles, *who's made a poo, eh, who's made a poo-poo, goo-goo, boo-boo.* . . . The baby happily waves its little legs, and mummy wipes the baby, lifts both its legs with one hand and kisses it. . . . *Who's kissing baby's bottom, hmm? Mummy's kissing it.* . . .

The scene in which the somewhat older baby drops his first little turd into the potty is equally familiar. The baby's act is usually accompanied by squealing approval from its surroundings, the baby's little turd is shown to the family, they joyfully congratulate the baby on its first victory. Using a potty for the first time is a symbolic act of joining the human race and entering into life as an individual. Not one of our acts in later life will provoke such tender and sincere expressions of love and delight. Still, although the poo-poo experience belongs to each of us individually, virtually none of us makes a connection between that experience and ourselves. What we remember are our children's and grandchildren's first performances, not our own.

Buli, however, remembers. Just as the inhuman strength of the monsters from fairy tales remains hidden and alters its form until it is in the end revealed in an unexpected place (in the heart of some little bird), so the strength of Buli's genius is hidden in a buried, distant fragment. The whole of Buli's life is subconsciously subordinated to just one aim, that of recreating that instant of absolute love from those around him, repeating the effect he achieved the first time he used the potty. The formula of that absolute happiness has been permanently imprinted in Buli's mind.

And that is why it is no accident that Buli chose literature as his field. And why Buli in his writer's life leans exclusively on women: a wife—that is, a woman who ensures the regularity of his literary production—women translators, voluntary promoters of his genius, analysts of his literary works, journalists, friends and admirers. At the same time, Buli is a kind of sexually indifferent hermaphrodite, the sexless king of a little imaginary kingdom, both eunuch and harem owner in one body. Buli never uses the full names and surnames of the women who surround him: he calls them Beba, Bibi, Boba, exactly like poo-poo, pronouncing the words with a kind of affectation, full of jokey patronizing warmth.

Actually no one in Buli's world uses a full name and surname, apart from Buli himself. If Buli says, "Sasha has just been here fixing our pipe!" Sasha could be a nickname for Buli's plumber, named after Alexander Pushkin. In Buli's world, Fedja is a nickname for Fyodor Dostoyevsky, Rob is Robert Musil, Bill is William Shakespeare. Buli (like every child) experiences himself as the center and his surroundings are made up of people whose names Buli joyfully distorts, reducing their height, size, and significance.

The secret of Buli's genius lies in the regularity of his literary production. He has an exclusively physical attitude to the creative process. The literary process is first consuming and then making. What he "eats" in the course of the day, he tidily "excretes" the next morning, before breakfast. Buli never interrupts the regularity of his digestion; that is why he lives the orderly life of a writer in his study. Buli subconsciously decided not to emerge from the infantile phase, at any price, so he quickly grasped that life itself is an over-complicated, spicy, and dangerous food that provides neither good digestion nor much longevity. That is why Buli consumes processed life—high-quality, premasticated—in a word, other people's books. Buli chooses the best brands of food. It does not occur to him to try unfamiliar, unrecognized, and untried products. If he has recently been referring to someone named Jim, that is a sure sign that his current menu includes Mr. Joyce.

Buli is not an ordinary parasite. He is not a tapeworm who settles in an organism, lives at its expense, but takes care not to devour its own house and destroy the organism which nourishes it. Buli uses his own stomach juices to transform other people's books into a mush, then excretes briquettes whose size always exceeds what he has eaten. All that remains of the works is an aura of geniality which through some unknown chemical reaction is transferred to Buli himself. Buli's digestion is perfect. No one has such teeth and such a stomach.

The secret of Buli's genius also lies in his reader. Buli is a fiction writer, but he rejects all the rules of fiction writing: thinking about that would only slow down his production. As a result, his readers are strangled by the vines of Buli's never-ending sentences before they can find in his "books" a plot, characters, dialogue, action, story. Buli's "books" are monumental monologues, tedious contemplation of the food he has devoured. It's hard to tell what kind of food is involved. But because Buli's monumental verbal briquettes usually have impressive titles—*Proust's Finger, Flaubert's Granny, Broch's Foot, Freud's Will, My Dinner with Walter Benjamin*—the reader has no choice but to attribute his confusion to Buli's hyper-erudition and his own incompetence.

How is it that the secret of Buli's genius lies in his reader, if no one reads Buli's "books"? That's just it! Buli's books are monuments to an obsessive literary bulimia. And monuments are not dismantled so that we can know what they're made of: monuments stand. That is why Buli's genius remains unquestioned. There is no one who would waste his time deconstructing it. Its deconstruction would take a whole lifetime.

It is true that from time to time Buli is ruffled by that image buried in his subconscious and he indignantly drives those around him to take a look at what he has done. His surroundings take his word for it, they mechanically express their admiration, no longer even glancing into the potty. There's nothing for Buli to do but accept it. He is consoled by the fact that his literature—whether or not it is admired—is assured eternity. If for no other reason than because of its monumental scale.

Buli gladly enquires of his fellow writers:

"So, have we done any paper-tormenting lately?" As might be expected, Buli uses the colloquial expression *to torment paper* or *to torture paper,* which means to write; *to torment a plate* in these languages means to eat reluctantly, without appetite.

His fellow writer, with obvious signs of creative constipation on his face, mutters through clenched teeth: "Well . . . not exactly. . . ."

Buli, like a person well satisfied with his health, adds cheerfully, "For me, thank goodness, it's every morning. That's how it was thirty years ago, and it's the same now. In just the last couple of months several hundred pages have piled up. . . . It's growing, I must say, *Mann's Mountain.*"

And Buli indifferently shifts his gaze from his interlocutor and directs it towards imagined distances where the outlines of snowy mountain peaks can be discerned. Among the peaks of the human spirit, his own mountain gleams. It is higher than the others. The fact that it is built of briquettes of recycled paper doesn't matter. Only mountaineers would know that, and there really aren't many mountaineers in the world.

1998

A Short Contribution to the History of a National Literature

The Top Ten Reasons to Be a Croatian Writer

To be a writer is not a particular blessing. To be the representative of a great literature is stimulating, but not the most agreeable sensation—a person is easily lost among giants. It is best to be a writer from a small country, especially if it is fresh and young. Being a Yugoslav writer was not bad, but to wake up one day as a Croatian writer, because that was the decision of a nation obsessed with the idea of its own state, that's the real jackpot!

Who are the Croats? Croatia is a small nation in the south of Europe whose inhabitants proudly beat the drum of their thousand-year history. They are known for having invented the tie: the story goes that the Croatian soldiers in Napoleon's army differentiated themselves by tying a dapper little ribbon round their necks, and the ribbon was then called "cravate" after the Croats. This is one of the best-known legends in the thousand-year history of the Croats. Another is connected with the "penkala," the ballpoint pen, which was invented in 1902 by Joseph Penkala (a Czech). Both these important pieces of information can be found in the advertising brochures of Croatia Airlines, the proud, high-flying Croatian aviation company.

In addition to their thousand-year history, the Croats have literacy, which began with a stone slab. The stone was carved in the eleventh century, discovered near a place called Baška, and is therefore known as the Baška Stone. The Croats are so proud of this beginning (the stone records the fact that someone is donating a field to the church) that nothing which has come since can surpass the significance of this symbol. So it turns out that other nations have a literature, while the Croats have a symbol. Models of the Baška Stone are sold as souvenirs, so that every tourist who takes a vacation on the Adriatic coast can buy this beginning for himself.

The Baška Stone, the dapper tie, and the ballpoint pen: no wonder Croatia has so many writers. At present, the Union of Croatian Writers has 536 members. Statistically, Croatia is a real paradise for writers. And not only statistically. Let us try to identify the main reasons why it is better to be a Croatian writer than any other kind of writer.

1. Because of the language

Definitely because of the language. Because it is a language which "thunders, rings, resounds, and sings," as a Croatian poet sang long ago. The Serbo-Croatian language spoken and written by Croats, Serbs, Bosnians, and Montenegrins is today officially divided into the Croatian, Serbian, and Bosnian languages. Honorable linguists do indeed affirm that the Croatian, Serbian, and Bosnian languages are just dialects with political significance, but, unfortunately, there are not many honorable linguists. However, this recent linguistic divorce has brought many advantages. Language, as "the substance of national identity" has become an affair of state, complete with Committees for the Defence of National Substance, and this development has given new importance to writers, for whom this substance is their stock in trade. Writers breathed a sigh of relief at the ebbing of competition: it is easier to be a writer in one's own village than in all three. It turns out that the Croatian writer can now be translated into Serbian and Bosnian and have an international career with hardly any effort at all. A large part of Croatia consists of Dalmatia, and people there speak a slightly different dialect; if this dialect also acquires political significance and becomes a language, Croatian writers will be able to use that "substance" too.

Although the linguistic possibilities within the Croatian language itself are great, some Croatian writers have also written in the language of the "occupiers," in Italian or Hungarian, and the occasional traitor even in Serbian.

As a result some writers, such as Ivo Andrić, have had two-thirds of their works thrown out of Croatian literature. He has remained a Croatian poet, but the Serbs and Bosnians are left to share him as a fiction writer and Nobel laureate.

The Croats love their language and when they do not know how to demonstrate to some foreigner the exceptional beauty of the Croatian language, they point to onomatopaeia and quote a couple of examples (*I cvrči, cvrči cvrčak na čvoru crne smrče,* "A cricket chirps on the knot of a black spruce"). The foreigners are won over instantly.

It is good to be a Croatian writer because of the importance of the language itself, because of its essential beauty, and because of onomatopaeia, which no other language in the world has in such abundance. Especially not Serbian.

2. Because of flexibility

The Croatian writer is a person with many different inclinations. That is why a Croatian writer can become president, which is not so exceptional if we accept the thesis that every president is in principle a poet. "When I was persecuted, and people even tried to assassinate me in a faked road accident, one foreigner said to me: You know, Professor-General, if you were not a Croat you would have won the Nobel Prize." So said Franjo Tudjman, the gifted Croatian writer and president, before he died. If not president, the Croatian writer today can easily find himself a job as a cultural attaché, because Croatia has more than a hundred and eighty embassies scattered through the world.

The Croatian cultural scene is dynamic and flexible, and that is why it is far more exciting there than elsewhere. For instance, I know an editor who became chief of police and a professor of aesthetics who became a paid state military adviser. I also know of several thieves who became humanists and several humanists who became thieves, writers who became war criminals and war criminals who became writers. I even know writers who have been erased from literary life because they wanted to be only writers.

It is good to be a Croatian writer because then your life is never dull.

3. Because of rejuvenation

The Croatian writer has a great advantage over other writers because Croatian literature is forever being rewritten from the beginning. The great Croatian national myth is the beginning of Croatian literacy, symbolized by the Baška Stone, so Croatian writers keep unconsciously returning to that stone.

Perhaps that is why in the young and fresh Croatian state the most valued profession is that of librarian. The Croats are profoundly aware that they must have a literature, above all because other European states have one—even the Serbs—so literature and culture are constantly in the vigilant eye of the Croatian cultural public. Librarians assiduously cleanse libraries of inappropriate, unfavorable, and outmoded books. For a living lesson in the revision, renovation, and refreshing of literary history, schoolchildren have sometimes been recruited to help librarians carry the books out to the trash.

In truth, it is far easier for Croatian writers to come to terms with their beginnings than sculptors, for instance. One Croatian sculptor, who turned out to be a Serb by nationality, had virtually all his sculptures, incautiously erected on Croatian soil, destroyed. The fact that the sculptor has an international reputation played no part in the collective decision of the local art fans to send his work back to the beginning.

Croatian writers often change their attitudes, opinions, and even biographies. If it is possible to say of any literature that it is not institutionalized, then one can say that of Croatian literature. It is sufficient, for example, for the minister of culture to announce publicly that he does not care for this or that writer and that writer is all but banned. Fellow writers gladly assist in this process of changing their colleagues' biographies. This is exceptionally thrilling and rejuvenating for the writers themselves.

4. Because of openness

The doors of Croatian literature have always been open to everyone. In Croatia today, there is an active Bosnian writer, a refugee from Sarajevo, to whom Croatia has given complete freedom of expression, and even two Serbian writers whose weekend houses on the Adriatic coast were not illegally occupied by anyone. It is true that one of them has a Croatian wife, the other a Croatian mother, but, as far as literature itself is concerned those are minor details.

The Croatian town of Pula earned its place in literary history by hosting James Joyce, who taught English there between November 1904 and March 1905. Thanks to Croatia, Joyce's physical appearance changed for the better: it was precisely in Pula that Joyce had his teeth fixed and went to a local barber to have his moustache trimmed in the latest local fashion. It is true that Joyce does not mention his stay in Pula much (apart from mentioning that he fixed his teeth and could now eat his favorite onion soup without discomfort), but from the Croatian side there is a rich vein of information about his stay. Croatian literature departments abound in scholarly studies in which Croatian writers stand side by side with James Joyce and other famous Irish writers, because Croatia and Ireland are small Catholic countries which have for centuries fought for independence and freedom from dubious and repressive federal structures. Croatia, thank goodness, has recently emerged, while Ireland is still suffering.

Another person who turned up in Croatia was Casanova, who caught gonorrhea in Vrsar. And then there's Gustav Aschenbach, a literary character, who on the way to his death in Venice set foot on the Croatian island of Brioni, later known for being Tito's retreat.

Although in America there is an Indian tribe called the Croatan—which had some difficulty in acquiring the status of Native Americans, because there are some indications that they are descended from Dalmatian sailors who went astray on the shores of North Carolina and "internationalized" with the local female population—it is hard for Croats to become American writers. Americans, however, can become Croatian writers whenever they feel like it. Julienne Eden-Bušić was an American terrorist who spent thirteen years in an American jail together with her Croatian husband, Zvonko Bušić-Taiko. In the biography of this important Croatian writer, there are two decisive dates. The first is the day in the 1970s when Julienne scattered leaflets from a Croatian skyscraper calling on the Croats to fight for their independence. The other is the day when, with her husband, she hijacked an airplane bound for New York (scattering the same leaflets on the way). An American policeman was killed. When she got out of prison, Julienne was promoted to Croatian citizen, granted recognition for her courage and for spreading the fame of Croatia abroad, and given the position of adviser at the Croatian embassy in Washington. Then Julienne returned to Croatia and got a job in a military unit responsible for the security of the president of the new Croatian state. In 1995 Julienne published an auto-biographical novel, *Lovers and Madmen,* which saw two editions in the Croatian language and received an important literary prize, also Croatian. The former American citizen lives as an acknowledged Croatian writer on the Adriatic coast, in a villa built for her by the Croatian army with Croatian taxpayers' money, working diligently on her new novel, *Lovers and Madmen, Part II.*

5. Because of mountaineering

It makes perfect sense that the Croats, as representatives of a small nation, are obsessed with size. When they talk, they like to use phrases such as "a spiritual colossus," "a moral rock," "a giant in spirit," "a Croatian titan." If any writer has a problem with low self-confidence, Croatia will take care of it.

The Croats often elevate their literature to the heights and use mountaineering metaphors to do so. But since they are, after all, a maritime people, the Croats often confuse their metaphors. This is how S. L., a prominent Croatian intellectual, professor of Croatian literature at Croatian and foreign universities, speaks of Croatian literature: "Just as a mother, almost invariably, prefers her backward child, fragile, weak, sickly, and placed in special classes, so too I, often, not always, but often, favor Croatian literature over the Himalayas to which I am directed by duty, intellect, and spirit. Croatian literature has its peaks, its lighthouses. Perhaps they are second-rate in comparison to the Himalayas, but they exist as a longing for the

Himalayas. The coldness, indifference, and haughtiness which stream naturally from the Himalayas must be borne calmly: if we persevere in our silent dialogue with the European heights, the time will come when the new lighthouses hear—of their own accord, almost without any external dialogue or propaganda—our Word, which will enrich them as well." Professor S. L. infects his students with a love of Croatian literature, carried along by one single idea: "Literature as such—as a phenomenon of the human spirit—has a vertical axis and, if you really want to establish a dialogue with it, it is accessed only by giants, only by Himalayas. Dostoyevsky was and remains one of my Himalayas," the professor adds.

6. Because of morality

Croatia is no Nepal. The capital city, Zagreb, prides itself on one skyscraper, a building with ten floors, which the inhabitants of Zagreb call The Skyscraper because of its height. So naturally Croats adore verticals. In speech they use phrases such as "spiritual vertical" or "moral vertical" with striking frequency. "Look at him, there goes a moral vertical," they say.

A typical example is that of the president of the Union of Croatian Writers. For almost ten years, as a "moral vertical," he demanded of writers that they should be "the moral conscience of their nation." Many people liked what he said, and hurried to be that "conscience" and that "vertical." Male writers, of course. No woman is ever proclaimed a vertical.

Incidentally, my public proposal that a cast of the vertically challenged president of the Union of Croatian Writers be made into a lifesize statue called The Moral Vertical—which every writer must keep on his desk as a reminder of what real literature should be—met with, surprisingly, no response. Maybe because most Croatian writers don't have a desk.

7. Because of significance

As part of their obsession with measuring size and significance, the Croatian daily *Morning Paper* sponsored a reader's poll inspired by *Time* magazine.

Time chose Albert Einstein as the person of the century; the Croatian person of the millennium was Tito. Miroslav Krleža, a man who himself wrote enough books for little Croatian literature to call itself a literature, took an excellent ninth place. Second place went to Franjo Tudjman, the Croatian president and another gifted writer. Gojko Sušak, a war criminal, took a modest nineteenth place, while another, bigger criminal, Ante Pavelić, was sixteenth.

Although most Croats do not like Mr. Krleža for what he wrote about them, although opportunists accuse him of opportunism, the semiliterate accuse him of erudition, and the untalented accuse him of a superfluity of talent, Croatian voters generously put their greatest writer in ninth place. Although the majority of Croats believe that not only books but every piece of paper except toilet paper *gathers dust,* Miroslav Krleža managed to take ninth place. It is good to be a Croatian writer because you have an excellent chance of taking the ninth place in the third millennium.

8. Because of sex

Croatian writers are predominantly male. It is sexy to be a Croatian writer. Their job, literature, makes Croatian male writers attractive, builds up their self-esteem, and gives them a sense of irreplaceability. And all that is very good for the sex life. Most Croatian writers change wives several times in the course of their lives, throwing the old ones out. Croatian writers are not only eternal, like all writers, but they also stay young for a long time. Forty-year-olds are called "our youngest writers," while fifty-year-olds are "representatives of the younger generation."

It is good to be a Croatian writer if you are a man. Croatian women writers are not sexy. They can become Croatian writers only if they are adaptable and very quiet.

9. Because of sex, again

A Croatian writer is actually two writers who go around together, a sadist and a masochist. That is why Croatian literature has always had two major themes: Croatian society unjustly destroys the nonconformist thinking individual, and Croatian society justly destroys the nonconformist thinking individual. The continuity of Croatian literature is due to the rich interplay between these two themes.

In the last ten years, a few thinking individuals have been thrown out of Croatian society, but other individuals have been integrated into Croatian society and even given space to think. One dead writer had his monument destroyed, but another dead writer had a monument erected to him. One writer had his house blown up, but another writer got a new house. Several writers have been threatened at gunpoint, publicly discredited in the media, had their names thrown out of school curricula and their works out of libraries, but other writers got their books published and their advances raised.

Unlike other literatures, which have developed within different literary movements, trends and styles—from classicism to postmodernism—Croatian literature has developed within its own, authentic literary movement called sadomasochism.

Croatian literary life is unusually stimulating.

10. Because of difference

The most important reason to be a Croatian writer is because then you're not a Serbian writer. The same holds true for Serbian writers—the best reason to be one is so as not to be Croatian. In fact, all of the top ten reasons why it's good to be a Croatian writer apply to Serbian writers. And Bosnian writers. And others as well.

2000

5 — ## Life without a Tail

"Somebody must have taken it," said Eeyore.
"How Like Them," he added, after a long silence.

The Writer in Exile

Dream

I live without papers, employment, assets, or permanent address.
—Darryl Pinckney

I had a dream. I was at an airport, waiting for someone. Finally the person I was waiting for, a woman of my age, appeared. Before we got into a taxi, I asked her "Don't you have any luggage?"

"No, I just have lifeage," said the woman.

The sentence my double had spoken could be translated: Life is the only luggage I carry with me.

Copyright

It seems proper that those who create art in a civilization of quasi-barbarism, which has made so many homeless, should themselves be poets unhoused and wanderers across language. Eccentric, aloof, nostalgic, deliberately untimely. . . .—George Steiner

In the twentieth century—a century of wars, persecution, terror, genocides, revolution, totalitarian systems, a century in which maps were changed, states and state borders were created and obliterated, a century of mass migrations—writers do not have a copyright on the theme of exile. Nevertheless, although they are statistically the most insignificant and unreliable witnesses, writers are those rare migrants who leave their footprints on the cultural map of the world.

127

A writer explores the theme from a position of double exile: as an actual exile and as a commentator on his own "condition called exile" (Brodsky). The writer tries to rationalize his personal nightmare in writing, to calm his exile's fears in writing, to put his broken life into some sort of shape through writing, to order the chaos he has landed in through writing, to fix the insights he has come to in writing, to dilute his own bitterness in writing. Perhaps because of that inner effort, an exile's writings are often marked by a particular kind of "coldness," which can be crudely compared to posttraumatic dissociation. An exile's writings are often "nervous," fragmented, explicitly or implicitly polemical, semantically polyvalent, ironic, self-ironic, melancholic, subversive, and nostalgic. This is because exile is itself a neurosis, a restless process of testing values and comparing worlds: the one we left and the one where we ended up. The exiled writer is torn by extremes: exile is a state of self-pity, but also of solitary rebellious audacity (Gombrowicz), a state of being drunk with freedom (Eberhardt), but of surreptitious resignation, exile is an "academy of intoxication" (Cioran), but also a "lesson in humility" (Brodsky).

Genre

> *Classically, exile was a punishment decreed from above, like the original sentence of banishment on Adam and Eve, which initiated human history.*—Mary McCarthy

Exile is a literary condition; it not only gives you a rich menu of literary quotes, but is a literary quote itself. The Christian history of the world begins with a story of exile. Exile is also the parable of the prodigal son, of betrayal, banishment, and condemnation, the myth of the double and role reversal, the myth of Odysseus, the story of Faust and Mephistopheles. Exile is a fairy tale about being thrown out of one's home, searching for home, and returning home; it is also a Russian fairy tale of Ivan the Fool, a parable about growing up, a romantic epic of individual revolt. It is an exceptionally appealing myth about metamorphosis.

Exile is also a style, a narrative strategy. A broken life can be told only in fragments (Rilke), "Certain literary genres and certain styles cannot, by definition, be practiced in exile"; the very state of exile, "by enforcing upon a writer several perspectives," favors genres and styles other than the traditional ones" (Milosz).

The reader accommodates the writer, and the exiled writer offers the reader his hand. It does not occur to the writer to discredit his own life story, nor would his reader forgive him that. So together author and reader create around the theme of exile an appealing aura of exclusivity. They not infrequently romanticize the theme of exile, as though it were a love story. And really, the genre of the love story and the genre of the exile's story are similar in one way: neither airs its own dirty laundry.

That is why, among other things, the important side of exile, the bureaucratic one, is always left in shadow. No one, not even the exile himself, wants to hear a story about painful encounters with bureaucracy, or consider whether Walter Benjamin might have killed himself just because he did not get his papers.

The real content of a love story is longing, and the story ends when the longing is fulfilled. A love story ends with marriage, the exile's when he acquires a passport from another country.

Decent people stay at home

Expect everything, you who are exiled. You are flung away, but you are not set free.—Victor Hugo

States do not like those who seek papers. Every state, of whatever kind, respects every other state; a bureaucrat respects a bureaucrat. That is why the emigré is punished by a lengthy, tortuous bureaucratic procedure in order to acquire a residence permit. Decent people don't abandon their states, or their old parents, just like that. Decent people stay at home.

Utopias of a world without frontiers, Khlebnikov's idea about poets having the right to a free room in any city of the world, huge migrations from worse worlds to better worlds, even nomadism as a lifestyle, even tourism—all end up facing the wall of bureaucratic regulations. And here, with the migrant's face against the wall, a new space opens up: a space of resignation and desperation, of fabrication and falsification, of mimicry and hypocrisy. Only fools piss into the wind, only stupid people make their broken lives more difficult, only the pigheaded test the extent of their rights. Only rebels become impatient towards every state, but rebels are a negligible minority. Pragmatists glide through the bureaucratic procedure without resistance, ordinary paper-seekers quietly achieve their rights, and the Mafia slides through borders like butter. The exiled writer, on the other hand, is often asked to explain publicly why he left his country. It turns out that for a criminal, "cosmopolitanism" is a lifestyle which goes with their job, while for the writer it is an exceptional life circumstance.

I myself am neither an emigré nor a refugee nor an asylum-seeker. I am a writer who at one point decided not to live in her own country anymore because her country was no longer hers.

Good girls go to heaven, bad girls go everywhere

When I lay claim to not being an exile or an uprooted drifter (although I am a vagabond), it is because I abhor the concept of exile, which goes clothed in the myth of romantic lamentation.—Breyten Breytenbach

I once watched with interest as a fellow writer of mine, East European, showed a journalist a photograph of his family. With deep emotion, he produced a picture in which he, his wife, and his child were sitting in a harmonious arrangement. He was lying. The people in the picture were his second wife and the child he had with her. The writer had since married a third wife and a third child was on the way. His desire to project an image of himself as a person with a normal life was so strong that we all believed it, including the writer himself.

What touched me in the whole episode was the scene of self-presentation. The writer had adapted his image to a generally accepted standard. He carried this picture everywhere with him because his first wife was too old (he was ashamed) and the first child too big (he was therefore old himself). The third wife was too young for him to seem serious in the eyes of those around him. The middle one was just right.

A woman writer in exile, single, with no children, who does not carry snapshots in her wallet, not even pictures of pets, occupies the lowest rung among exiled writers. Because decent women stay at home.

That is presumably why, when I was leaving Zagreb, my mother thrust into my hand a little album the size of a wallet, full of family photographs which she had selected.

"Take this with you," she said. "So that you have something to show, when people ask. . . . So they don't think you're alone in the world. . . ."

The exile as a projection screen

Exile brings you overnight where it would normally take a lifetime to go.
—Joseph Brodsky

The exiled writer is not met with indifference. His life's choice, exile, provokes not only the people in the environment he leaves but also the people in the environment where he ends up. The political aspect of exile is something which everyone expects from a writer, and which is therefore boring; what makes exile attractive is the idea of exile itself. The idea of self-banishment secretly intrigues everyone. Exile is a total change, achieving a different life, realizing the daydream of how it would be to wake up one day in a different town, in a different country, perhaps as another person. Exile is a kind of coveted trial: we all have a hidden longing to test ourselves in the exam of life. Exile is that dream of transformation.

Surrogates of exile

Good old exile ain't what it used to be.—Joseph Brodsky

Contemporary man, finally abandoned by God and ideologies, left to get by on his own as best he can, has only one thing left: himself, his naked human body. Having achieved "practical freedom" (Baudrillard), man does not seem to understand whether an encounter with himself ought to be cause for euphoria or resignation, because it seems that what contemporary man would most like to do with his new freedom is to avoid himself. Today's culture is obsessed with the idea of self-banishment and expresses this idea in numerous ways. Cultural obsessions with the invention and reinvention of the self are nothing other than signs that man feels confined in his own skin. The longing for another life is socially legitimized and stimulated by the media, and, of course, by industries always ready to satisfy the desires of their consumers.

Medicine, especially plastic surgery, has become a magic medium of transformation for contemporary man, and its variations on the theme of personal reinvention are numerous and imaginative. A certain Cindy Jackson underwent dozens of operations in order to change her appearance to resemble a Barbie doll. A New York woman endured numerous operations in order to resemble as closely as possible her beloved Siamese cat.

The cultural obsession with physical transformation (and our body is all that we have at our disposal) is satisfied by gyms, the diet industry, techniques of sculpting the body, and, of course, fashion. "You're entitled to be whatever you want to be," says Ralph Lauren, promoting the idea that self-creation is in fact the last stage of human liberation.

The cultural obsession with "spiritual" transformation is satisfied by all kinds of gurus, happiness pills, and handbooks about how to become different, how to change. The profession of psychotherapist has been replaced by a new one: "coaches" manage personal lives, suggest life changes, direct personal life episodes.

The longing for a change of scene is no longer satisfied by tourism (also a surrogate of exile), but by an imaginative surrogate: architecture. The Disneyfication of America, and increasingly also of Europe, is confirmed by stores such as Nikeland, a multimedia commercial temple to sneakers, as well as hotels, theme parks, and shopping malls in which "consumers are transformed into immigrants. The system in which they move about is too vast to be able to fix them in one place, but too constraining for them ever to be able to escape from it and go into exile elsewhere" (Michel de Certeau).

At the end of the twentieth century, man has become his own favorite toy. And he occupies himself in making and remaking, inventing and reinventing himself. So all the great utopias and revolutions have today merged into one: revolutionizing the idea of one's own body, one's own image, one's own person.

Exile is a life choice, and not a role-playing game. What still distinguishes the exile from the tourist and the player in the modern game of reinventing the self is the definitiveness of exile. If that were not the case, we would all be in exile.

A true exile never returns

Our fatherland is in exile.—Miguel de Unamuno

The true exile never returns, even when he can, even when the hurt called the "homeland" is healed. Why repeat the same journey? Few have the strength for two exiles.

I once asked Joseph Brodsky whether he would ever go back to Russia, at least for a visit. Instead of replying, he showed me a letter. It was a little, crumpled letter, in Russian, with a vile anti-Semitic message. Its anonymous sender warned the writer never to think of returning home.

"How can I go back after this?" said Brodsky.

What surprised me was the pathos of his reaction—not its meaning, but the way it was expressed. Because Brodsky was certainly not among the "performers of exile."

Later, in a book of interviews with the poet, I came across a touching detail. When a journalist had asked him the same question, Brodsky had shown him the same letter.

The famous exile evidently needed some obstacle. He did not know how to, or simply did not want to, explain his own unease, his confused emotions, maybe simply his weariness with an already worn-out story. So Brodsky responded to every question about his return to Russia with a prepared item from a pathetic pantomime with an ostensibly conclusive key argument: a stupid, crumpled, anonymous letter.

Because of sausages

"Fixed up," established in the comfort of his fall, what will he do next? He will have a choice between two forms of salvation: faith and humor.—E. M. Cioran

An acquaintance of mine, a Russian writer who emigrated during the Cold War, was exceptionally warmly welcomed in Western Europe. In numerous interviews, he stretched out, like chewing gum, a metaphor about "communism which like a vampire sucks the blood of its adherents" until he himself grew bored with it.

"I emigrated because of sausages," he said in the end.

"How do you mean?"

"In Russia, there are no sausages."

My acquaintance, in other words, performed a public act of personal deheroization. And soon he was left in peace, because he pigheadedly refused to abandon his story of the sausages. He published his books, which were unjustly neglected. The media like heroes.

Exiles are not like us

For better or worse, you are an outsider.—Breyten Breytenbach

I was once invited to an academic conference, and I was glad that I would be talking in front of colleagues. I was like you, I said, explaining that I had worked at a university for many years.

There was an immediate ripple of dissatisfaction among the participants. Without realizing it, I had made a social gaffe. Exiles are permitted many things, but not to be like *us,* like *normal,* orderly people. Because *we* have paid a high price for our *normal,* orderly life, but nobody cares about *us.*

One person in the audience said that my exile was not true exile, because I had a passport, I was free to return to my country, it wasn't like they had beaten me up or put me in prison, had they? I should call my exile by its true name: extended tourism.

Another participant, a Czech, shouted that he had fled to Germany from communism, while, by all accounts, I had run away from post-communism, from democracy. I should not discredit the honorable tradition of East European exiles.

All in all, exiles like to see their own exile as the only dignified moral choice. That is why they cannot bear to have their *tragic* destiny compared with other exiles' destinies. And those who are not exiles cannot admit the possibility that exiles were once people like them, because if they were, how could they now be exiles?

Exiles don't live up to your expectations
Exile is a jealous state.—Edward Said

A West European writer once told me: "But surely you'll go back some day, won't you?"

"Why should I?" I asked.

The writer was speechless. While she herself spends six months a year in Spain and the other six in France, which she feels is quite normal, for me she had ordained a return to my homeland. Why had this West European writer gotten it into her head to send me back? Because I was an *East European* writer. And East European writers do not live in the West, unless they have to. An American writer in Berlin, a German writer in Ireland, a Dutch writer in Portugal—all of them live the life which is expected from people of their profession. A Romanian writer living in Paris, without a clear political reason, is *suspect.*

The exile is the screen onto which we project our fantasies of exile, and as long as he lets us do this, he is welcome. He is welcome as someone who has *suffered*, as a *victim of the régime*, a *fighter for democracy*, a *lover of freedom* who couldn't stand oppression in the country he left. As soon as he steps out of his stereotype, he becomes undesirable, because he has betrayed our expectations. We express our sympathy, and he, ungrateful creature, bites the hand that pets him.

The exiled writer sometimes feels like a racehorse. His friends, people who are dissatisfied with their own lives, well-meaning fans, other exiles, everyone bets on him. For exile is at the same time a dream of freedom:

freedom from things, from family, from banal everyday life. The exile is living proof that an independent, creative, and dynamic life does exist. But nobody asks how the exile earns his freedom and what price he pays for it. Because the exile is someone else's projection. As well as his own.

Exile is a lesson in adaptation

Our man is a little bit corrupt, almost by definition.—Joseph Brodsky

Exile is usually a voluntary choice. Politically intolerable situations are typically tolerated: most people stay and adapt to the circumstances. The exile is a person who refuses to adapt.

If we accept the thought that exile is the result of a failure to adapt, that the exile is therefore a kind of asocial and disturbed person, then in exile the exiled person is faced with the tragicomedy of his situation. For life in exile is a process of adaptation.

Having left my country because I could not adapt to the permanent terror of lies in public, political, cultural, and everyday life, I meet my compatriots abroad, and many of them lie just like the ones who stayed at home. Yugoslav exiles (as long as they are not refugees) often lie because of some administrative detail: namely, none of them has been deprived of his passport. Those who have stayed at home also lie, because many of them could have crossed the frontier with that same passport. The impossibility of returning to their homeland gave the Cold War East European exiles an aura of tragedy. The possibility of return deprives Yugoslav exiles of this aura.

Exiled writers have an additional problem of self-presentation, because they are asked to articulate publicly their *condition called exile*. On the other hand, no one asks an exhausted Muslim woman from Bosnia with five little children anything, because everything is obvious.

With time, exiled writers touch up their own biographies (according to the demands of the environment in which they happen to be); they write hagiographies about their own exile, because that is what is expected of them, and they do not mind. With time, many adapt to the stereotypical image that those around them have of exile. Many accept their role in the sociogenre.

Among the not-so-numerous Yugoslav intellectuals-in-exile, there are those who gladly stress their role in the struggle against Serbian or Croatian nationalism (without omitting to mention that they had been victims of communism as well), although in fact they ended up abroad because they did not want to fight. There are those who publicly maintain that they ran away from their *dictators,* although maybe they actually ran away from their wives. There are those who claim that they ran away from nationalism but, when invited to, gladly accept the role of representing their national literature abroad. They have learned the lesson: it is easy to perform anti-nationalism, but difficult to remain a-national. Even Western Europe will not tolerate the nationally indifferent: the proud West European ideology of multiculturalism wants declared ethnic cultural identities in order to generously grant them the freedom of self-realization.

All in all, suspicious of states and societies (because life has taught them to be) many exiles have one foot in one state and the other in a different one. You never know when you might need one. So exile, the alleged defection from local lies, is transformed into a new lie. With time, exiled persons adapt themselves to the image which they believe is expected of them. They cannot help but remind you of professional entertainers who know their audience well.

The exiled writer and his "homeland"

Above all, do not complain. They would laugh. After the complaint, the abuse would start again, same as before, without any variation; why bother to change slime?—Victor Hugo

It is rare that people leaving their familiar surroundings do so with the clear idea that they are leaving forever. Forever or not, for the exile the surroundings he has left (and not an abstract "homeland") remain a traumatic zone.

The surroundings they have abandoned rarely forgive exiled writers. The fact that, before he left, they had burned him in effigy, spat in his face, attacked him publicly, made normal life impossible for him, threatened him, called him in the middle of the night to drive him out of the country, published his phone number in the papers so that others could do the same (and others did, with gusto), the fact that they erased him from public life, put him on blacklists, prevented him from publishing, that they publicly humiliated him, excluded him from their ranks, threw his books out of public libraries and school curricula, that they proclaimed him *a traitor to the homeland, an enemy of the nation,* the fact that this was all done by colleagues and friends with whom he had worked and associated for some twenty years (all of which, incidentally, happened to me)—none of this counts. The exile's departure is simply proof that they were right.

Those who stay will never lose interest in those who leave—all tormentors remain drawn to their victims. Those who stay stick stubbornly to their point of view, convinced that the writer is not only *a traitor of the homeland,* but that he is now living well from selling that same *homeland* all over the world. He is even making money out of them, in other words, on top of everything else.

"What do you mean, making money?" the exiled writer asks, in his imagined conversations with people "back home."

"You sell our homeland all over the world!"

"I couldn't even if I wanted to. Our homeland is small and insignificant. It would be like trying to sell Albanian chewing gum!"

"How come?"

"No one buys it."

"The CIA will always buy it!" his countrymen insist, unmoved, firmly convinced of both their importance on the geopolitical map of the world and the CIA's solvency.

The fact that the homeland is commercially worthless is the greatest insult an exile can send back home. And the fact that the exiled writer did not die when he left, that he is not only still alive but still earning, drives the people back home completely mad.

With time, the gulf which both the *exile* and the *abandoned* believe will disappear grows even wider. The home environment nurtures its fantasies about the life of the exile and an image of itself as victim. Because they live where they live, and it does not occur to them to leave (decent people stay at home!), they are the ones who are burning themselves out on the battlefield for democracy twenty-four hours a day, and not waving a little article published in a foreign newspaper, like *some people*. They work hard and are barely able to make ends meet, while *some people* make a living out of their suffering.

The exiled writer—who just for a moment had hoped to relax a little in his role of "victim" and cry on the shoulder of his one remaining friend, to complain without restraint in his own language, to describe his struggle for survival, who hoped that he could finally list all the insults heaped on him *abroad*—has no choice but to pick up his things and head back where he came from, back into exile.

Those who have left their home because of nationalism would do well to remember that nationalism and exile are inseparable, just because they do not go together at all. The exile ought to remember that with his departure he has rated individualism higher than collectivism, that he has preferred a "fundamentally discontinuous state of being" (Said) to a false national continuity, that he has, therefore, preferred the freedom of rootlessness to "roots" and "cradles," that what he has run away from are precisely their "founding fathers, their basic, quasi-religious texts, their rhetoric of belonging, their historical and geographical landmarks, their official enemies and heroes" (Said), that he has, therefore, of his own free will, abandoned that stubborn, exclusive, self-intoxicated, aggressive noise of the isolated tribe ready to throw stones at the first person who is different from them.

The writer in the trap of a tragicomic paradox

> *If one were to assign the life of an exiled writer a genre, it would have to be tragicomedy.*—Joseph Brodsky

Having freed himself from his homeland, the exiled writer suddenly realizes that he is caught in a tragicomic trap. Once outside the country he has abandoned, his only identity is that of a representative of that country.

Although I no longer exist in Croatia as a Croatian writer, I am elsewhere labeled a Croatian writer almost without exception. Not by my choice,

I have become a *more Croatian* Croatian writer than I would have been had I stayed in Croatia. In other words, I have become what I am not.

Why does the rest of the world label me a Croatian writer? Because it simply does not know how else to label me. Everyone is someone's writer, everyone belongs to some nation, everyone writes in some language, why trouble oneself with a statistically insignificant example of the dysfunction of national identities?

Behind every writer stands his homeland. Invitations to literary gatherings with the names of the participants resemble lists of competitors in the Olympics: there is always the name of a country in parentheses. Only once did I see the word *transnational* in parentheses after the name of a writer and I immediately envied him. At literary gatherings I feel as though I were at the Eurovision song contest and am suddenly anxious that after my reading or talk I will hear a gong and a voice announcing: Croatia, five points! I dream that one day I shall remove the stickers that other people have assiduously attached to me and become just my name. Because that, just a name, is the greatest literary recognition that any writer can earn. For everyone else: Cyprus, five points; Poland, two points; Belgium, ten points. . . .

The advantages of exile

To be alone, to be poor, in need, to be ignored, to be an outsider who is at home everywhere, and to walk, great and by oneself, toward the conquest of the world.—Isabelle Eberhardt

Exile is a voluntary job of deconstructing the established values of human life. The exile, like it or not, tests the basic concepts around which everyone's life revolves: concepts of home, homeland, family, love, friendship, profession, personal biography. Having completed the long and arduous journey of battling with the bureaucracy of the country where he has ended up, having finally acquired papers, the exile forgets the secret knowledge he has acquired on his journey, in the name of life which must go on.

Nermina, a housewife, had lived her whole life in Sarajevo. She brought up two daughters, lost her husband, and then along came the war. One daughter escaped to London, the other went with her own daughter to America. Both did well. Hana registered for postgraduate studies in London and completed a doctorate; Senada was given a green card in an assistance package for Bosnian refugees, enrolled her daughter in a university, and got herself a job at the Los Angeles airport. Nermina refused to leave Sarajevo. "No one is going to drive me away, I will live, or die if I have to, where I was born." But when the Dayton Accords finally ended the shelling, Nermina announced that peace was far more difficult than war and set off to be with her daughter in L.A.

In her sixty-sixth year, for the first time in her life, Nermina crossed the border of Yugoslavia, the country where she was born, and with the passport of a new country, Bosnia, landed on American soil. As soon as Nermina landed, her daughter complained that life in America was alienated (that was the word she used, "alienated") and that she intended to go back to Sarajevo.

Nermina stayed. A government organization found her a little apartment, gave her a little social assistance. They registered her in a course of English for foreigners. In this class, among Mexicans, Koreans, Bosnians, among "all sorts," Nermina began a new life. She turned out to be an excellent student. She was given a little diploma. She framed the diploma. She did not abandon her studies; on the contrary, she is carrying on. Everybody at school likes her. Whenever she goes to class she brings fresh homemade Bosnian pies and feeds the Mexicans, Koreans, and Bosnians. Sometimes she calls her daughter in London and says in English, not without pride: "This is your mother, Nermina, speaking. How are you?"

Anxious Hana, from whom I heard the story, visited her mother, trying to persuade her to go back to Sarajevo. Nermina refused.

"But what will you do in this far-off world? You have no family here!"

"I can't go back," said Nermina. "I'm going to school. Besides, what would all my Mexicans, Koreans, and Bosnians do without me and my pies. . . ?"

In her apartment, a little replica of their Sarajevo apartment, Nermina continued, "You know, Hana, from here it seems to me that I spent my whole life decorating and cleaning that apartment of ours in Sarajevo. And here I have all the same things: Rico brought me a second-hand TV, Kim this fridge, and Sevdo dragged up this sofa. . . ."

In an instant (because she doesn't have time to dawdle), Nermina achieved for the first time a kind of personal freedom, and was now reconciled with her life.

I tell this story to my compatriots whenever they complain that they are having a hard time (and they complain all the time, that's what people are like, what can you do!). And I tell this story to myself whenever I am tempted to complain that I am having a hard time.

The physics and metaphysics of exile

For the other truth of the matter is that exile is a metaphysical condition.
—Joseph Brodsky

On a brief trip to San Antonio, I visited the famous Alamo museum. Rummaging through the museum souvenir shop, I came across a children's book whose title I liked. The book celebrated a certain "Savior of Alamo" and *Her Life Story: Presented through the Clothes She Wore.*

I could describe my nomad-exile's life through the objects I keep buying over and over again (coffee pots, household devices, can openers, hair dryers with 120W to 220W converters, CD players, plugs and adapters for my computer, slippers), because I always leave them behind. My story could be told by my suitcases and bags, which I drag after me, which keep dragging themselves after me, which I leave behind before buying new ones. My exile's life could be told by visiting cards with names which no longer denote real people, because I have forgotten who they are. My exile's life could be told by the numerous visas and stamps in my passport, bills, piles of papers which prove that I was somewhere, that I bought something somewhere, that I signed something somewhere, although with time this so-called proof corresponds less and less to my memory.

All in all, if by some miracle this heap of things were to appear in front of me, I would probably be terrified by the nightmare of my personal life. Constantly building and dismantling a new home, packing and repacking, the ever wearier repetition of this ritual as though it were a computer game and not real life, establishes a special kind of connection between the exile and his own biography. Living the visible, bare physicality of exile, the exiled person develops a different perception of space and time than the perceptions of ordinary life.

In Berlin, coming out of the subway, I saw an elderly Bosnian woman in baggy trousers, looking around her in bewilderment at a crossroads and murmuring, "Oh God, where am I?" The exile has more opportunities to ask himself that question than other people. That is his privilege, but also the source of a profound personal terror.

Exile as destiny

Taking this route for an exiled writer, in many ways, is like going home— because he gets closer to the set of ideals which inspired him all along.
—Joseph Brodsky

The exile, if nothing else, has time for browsing through his own biography. The exile digs through his own past looking for an explanation of what is happening to him in the present. The exile wonders which came first, the chicken or the egg: did his exile not begin long before he really left, and is not this current state called exile only the realization of some distant dream?

Exile is a child's fairy tale about the cap which makes you invisible, *shapka-nevidimka*. One day, the idea which intoxicated the child's imagination became the reality of exile. For exile is a voluntary journey into anonymity, it is catapulting yourself into the margins, into voyeurism, into invisibility.

Just as once, in my distant childhood, I was excited by the cap of invisibility, I was later excited by Antonioni's film *The Passenger,* a story for grown-ups about roughly the same thing. Stealing a dead man's passport in a hotel and putting it into his pocket, the main character (Jack Nicholson) changes his identity and is soon trapped in the destiny of the dead man. Antonioni's hero, like the hero of the existential genre called exile, cannot ever go back, cannot ever simply take off the cap and make everything the way it was again.

There, at that point of impossibility of return, begins a kind of intimacy between the exile and his own "destiny."

The writer's final meeting with the exile in himself

> *The fox is the god of cunning and treachery. If the spirit of the fox enters a man, that man's descendants will be cursed. The fox is the writer's god.*
> —Boris Pilnyak

There are exiles who, once they leave, having burned all their bridges behind them, become *wild people.* The exile finds it hard to part from the freedom he has acquired, his senses become more acute, he becomes sensitive to every possible trap. He angrily removes every label from himself and refuses to be classified in any way, to be reduced to a representative of the country whose passport he possesses, to be a member of any family. In a word, he becomes a difficult person, a *pain in the neck.* He refuses to be domesticated. With time, he develops the instinct of an animal, he becomes an *outlaw,* he keeps changing his lair, he is hard to catch. If he does settle down, he becomes a stranger in his own home, with a packed suitcase always waiting by the door. He becomes someone who breaks norms, he itches at all constraints, he becomes accustomed to a life outside the normal order. With time he merges with his own alienated face. He becomes an *enemy,* a *traitor;* he moves *underground,* where he was once driven; he becomes subversive, because he was once accused of subversion; he becomes a renegade, because he was once accused of being one.

At a certain point, the writer meets the exile in himself and is reconciled. The condition called exile indeed becomes his true state. Having gone in a circle, the writer returns to his true *home.*

It was Russian avant-garde culture that most passionately took up the idea of the artist as traitor and the artistic work as treachery. This culture elaborated rich strategies of the betrayal of established artistic principles and literary traditions. Art had untouchable autonomy, and all means were permitted in the defence of that autonomy. The fundamental artistic procedure of Russian avant-garde literature was defamiliarization, *otstrannenie,* estrangement, the betrayal of readers' expectations. In that sense the writer was a traitor and the metaphor of betrayal was the trademark of the true work of art.

Double exile

The homeland? Why, every eminent person was a foreigner even at home just because of that very eminence. Readers? Why, they never wrote "for" readers anyway, always "against" them. Honors, success, renown, fame: why, they became famous precisely because they valued themselves more than their success.—Witold Gombrowicz

Finding himself in the contemporary literary marketplace, the exiled writer with his adopted set of "treacherous" artistic principles gradually realizes that he has actually ended up in a double exile. For the "artists of literary exile" are precisely the writers whom the literary market understands least. Otherwise, it wouldn't be a market, just as publishing would not be called the publishing industry. The literary market demands that people adapt to the norms of production. As a rule, it does not tolerate disobedient artists, it does not tolerate experimenters, artistic subversives, performers of strange strategies in a literary text. It rewards the artistically obedient, the adaptable, the diligent, those who respect literary norms. The literary market does not tolerate the old-fashioned idea of a work of art as a unique, unrepeatable, deeply individual artistic act. In the literary industry, writers are obedient workers, just a link in the chain of production.

Our exiled writer suddenly realizes that he has ended up in exile with an old craft which died out long ago and which no one needs. The tragicomedy of his position is multiplied. He left his repressive environment in order to preserve himself as a writer, and has ended up in another such environment, under the repressive rules of the book market. In the end, the writer faces the last paradox: good writers feel banished wherever they are, and only bad writers feel at home everywhere.

The exiled writer is condemned to marginality, even if he wins the Nobel Prize (like Brodsky), even if he happens to fall into the mainstream of popular culture (like Nabokov), even if chance brings him fame. Some (like Solzhenitsyn) are driven by their marginality to return to their literary homelands. Because only the environment which gave them their wounds knows how to cure them, only it knows how to boost the writer's shattered ego, wave the writer's name like a national flag, let him feel his importance, teach him in school, bury him with due honors, build a statue of him, name a street after him.

The exiled writer finds himself in a snare of intoxicating and frightening freedom. That freedom implies acceptance of marginality and isolation. In choosing exile, he has chosen loneliness.

Life is a dream

Does God try to remind us, somewhat brutally, that exile is the permanent human condition?—Leszek Kolakowski

Every Saturday I call my mother in Zagreb. We have a little routine. For some reason my mother is always interested in what time it is in the country I am phoning from. We compare the weather, we talk a little about life. Mother, who has not left Zagreb for years, recently said with a sigh, "You know, my life does not seem to be mine. I don't know whose life I'm living, I only know I'm not living my own."

I was speechless and didn't know how to answer. My mother had spoken the authentic sentence of an exile.

Return to the homeland

In a century of Displaced Persons and exiles and those fleeing famine or torture, you are in a position to share and contribute to an historically important, and vital, human experience. . . . Take heart then. Lady Luck has smiled upon you!—Breyten Breytenbach

In school, I was enchanted by my very first reading book. It was the brightly colored pictures that did it. I quickly learned the letters, but those pictures, they were my first thrilling information about a world full of strong, clear colors. My socialist primer promoted "brotherhood and unity among the nations and nationalities of Yugoslavia." The pictures showed little people dressed in different kinds of clothes: some had fezes on their heads, others caps, still others hats, some had peasant shoes, others boots. I did not see the little people from the primer in real life until later, at folklore festivals. I suppose that is why I grew up believing that people were all the same, they just wore different costumes. My later travels to various parts of Yugoslavia did not convince me that its inhabitants were "an interweaving of various nations and nationalities," as my primer had taught me, but even though I never managed to get to know anyone with a fez on his head, I accepted the rules from my primer and tried to respect the difference between a fez and a cap.

My socialist primer also taught me that "all the people on the globe" were "brothers," "white, yellow, and black." The little pictures of children colored yellow, black, and white particularly caught my imagination. But I could never find black or yellow children in real life, not in Yugoslavia.

Yugoslav propaganda about a multiethnic and multicultural society turned out to be unconvincing, especially much later, when the cap, the fez, and the hat went to war, maintaining that they could not live together. Then I defended Yugoslav multiculturalism. Soon the idea not only was trampled underfoot by the war, but collapsed of its own accord in a foreign refugee camp, where Yugoslav refugees not infrequently refused to be placed with others just as wretched, but of a different color.

Exile, then, becomes a return to a retro-utopia, to the pictures from some old primer. Today I really am surrounded by brothers, black and yellow and white, in New York, Berlin, London, Paris, Amsterdam. . . . I catch, infallibly, a spark of recognition, I know my kind. I nod my head and smile. Their belief in a better life does not permit me to slide into cynicism, their effort to survive makes me more modest, their marginality subdues my "appetite for recognition" (Brodsky). Sometimes, like my mother, I feel that I do not know whose life I am living, but I quickly forget the thought. . . . It must after all be mine, my "lifeage."

There's no place like home

During the twenty years of Odysseus' absence, the people of Ithaca retained many recollections of him but never felt nostalgia for him. Whereas Odysseus did suffer nostalgia, and remembered almost nothing.—Milan Kundera

Dorothy's exile doesn't begin at the beginning of her journey, when a powerful hurricane takes her away from Kansas, but at the very end, at home, when, overexcited, she tries in vain to tell the adults gathered round her bed what she experienced in Oz. The adults nod their heads and smile, but do not believe her. When Dorothy realizes that she won't be able to tell her story—when she gives up—she utters one of the most quoted phrases of all time: "There's no place like home." An attentive listener can hear more than a little disappointment mixed in with the reconciliation: Dorothy accepts the "reality" of adults, not because she herself believes it but simply because she is a polite girl. At least that's how it is in the movie. In L. Frank Baum's book the phrase is less excited: "I'm so glad to be at home again!"

My other favorite story about exile is the first one. I can easily imagine Lilith, the serpent and first woman of knowledge, offering the apple from the Tree of Life and whispering in Eve's ear a simple slogan: "Good girls stay in heaven, bad girls go everywhere."

That's why when the Croatian president euphorically proclaimed Croatia "paradise on earth" in the early 1990s, I knew what I had to do. I took an apple and got on the first train leaving the country. I only later realized that I had completely forgotten about Adam. He's probably still there.

1999

War Is War,
but Intellectuals Are Only Human

War is show business!—Wag the Dog

1.

The happy parents gave birth to a little boy. Everything was going well, but after a while it turned out that the boy was mute. The unhappy parents did everything in their power, but then, poor things, they just had to accept it.

Then, during a family meal when the boy was five years old, he suddenly spoke.

"Pass the salt, please," he said.

His parents burst into tears of happiness. "You can talk! Why haven't you ever said anything before!?"

"Because I didn't need anything."

I remembered this joke recently, during the lively involvement of intellectuals in the media discussion about whether NATO should bomb Yugoslavia. I wondered whether to get involved myself or to keep quiet like the little boy. In the end, I decided to do both, and only undercut myself in the process.

In the last ten years, during the collapse of Yugoslavia and the ensuing war, I have learned something about human nature. I have also learned something about my own kind, writers. I'm not saying that other kinds of people appeal to me more, but one should put one's own house in order first.

As far as local (Croatian, Serbian, Bosnian, Slovenian . . .) representatives of the intelligentsia are concerned, I wouldn't say that they exactly enchant me. In fact, most of them annoy me.

The ones I find most annoying are the loud ones, the *drummers,* the ones who put their writerly skills at the service of their governments, politicians, and military men, as though they were waiters instead of writers. They disguise themselves as defenders of the *ethnic substance,* of cultural identity. They think that art and literature without *ethnic substance* is postmodern trash. Their books usually have titles like *The Heart of the Fatherland* or *The Womb of the Motherland.* They get bigger apartments or houses from their new governments, important jobs in the media, or diplomatic service in various countries. Many choose exotic ones.

I am no more enamored of *warrior-writers,* the ones who take the question of commitment literally and can hardly wait to throw down the heavy burden of their pens to take up a rifle. They usually write poetry, perhaps because poetry is more adaptable to a mobile life at the front. After their return from the front, they find themselves on the payroll of obscure military institutions, although they really wanted to be Minister of Culture. Unlike their pregnant poetry, their later dutiful scholarly works bear lazy titles such as *The Role of Writers in Defending the National Idea during the Homeland War, 1991-93.* The years in the title vary, because every side has its own idea of when the Homeland War started and ended.

There's nothing much to love in the silent ones, either, the ones who are *neither fish nor fowl.* You never know what they are thinking, and in the end they always turn out to have been right. They usually disguise themselves as defenders of so-called pure art and are ostensibly disgusted by any political involvement. This devotion to pure art means that their bibliography is usually thin, and their books regularly bear minimalist titles: *Splinters, Gleanings, Motes.* These people receive little from their new governments and never understand why.

Then there are the dissidents, the most dynamic group of writers, and I don't like them either. The ones who open their mouths first, the *impulsive individualists,* fare worst. They lose everything and usually end up in exile.

In the meantime, everyone forgets what it was that the impulsive individualists said, so their exile is viewed as a prolonged vacation abroad. With
time, they become misanthropic. They are natural losers. No one likes them,
even though they were right all along.

The ones who open their mouths at the right moment fare better, the
shrewd individualists with a more precise sense of political timing. They leap
into dissidence just when the personal risk is minimal. They not only keep
what they had—property, homeland, and an honorable position at home—
but also are seen abroad as optimistic fighters for democracy. Everyone likes
them, because everyone likes optimists and people in power, and the shrewd
are the future people in power.

When the time comes, when the smell of political change is in the air,
many other people turn out to be dissidents too: transformed criminals, converted nationalists and communists, fascists and antifascists, political passers-
by and tourists, those who have converted from *fish* to *fowl* or the other way
around. Some move into temporary exile just to be closer to the foreign
media, in case they have to make some statement or comment on things, for
they have learned that the war hasn't ended and that it's time for them to
make a profit too. Such people spend the winter in exile and the summer in
their villas on the Adriatic coast.

The fact that the local intelligentsia give little cause for comfort doesn't mean
that the outsiders are better. In the past ten years, there have been intellectual stars on all the warring sides—defenders, spokesmen, bearers of state
medals, *our best friends abroad,* from the French philosopher Alain
Finkielkraut, intellectual superstar of the Croats, to his fellow philosopher
HBL (Bernard-Henry Levy), nimble promoter of the Bosnians, to the Austrian writer Peter Handke, fierce defender of the Serbs.

I cannot say that the political commitment of these foreign intellectuals
is merely a gesture without any personal risk, or a harmless investment of
time which they calculate will bring them significant moral credit. That
would not be just. I cannot accuse them of interfering in other people's
business either, because every thinking individual has the right to interfere,

including intellectuals. It would be unfair to say that an "imperial nostalgia" or a longing for a "Balkan Express" thrill is the hidden motive for their political involvement. I cannot say that their "colonial" arrogance prevents them from understanding anything, because such an accusation is simply the self-consoling arrogance of the colonized. In fact, anything I might say is wrong. Maybe these intellectuals speak simply because they are asked to. The siren song of the media is hard to resist. Intellectuals are only human, and everyone needs to be needed.

All in all, the war in former Yugoslavia quickened the mental, moral, and emotional pulse of European intellectuals. The long-since-moribund came to life, emerged from hibernation, and sprang once again into their traditional role, which in former times had been a source of bitter moral compromise but also sweet moral satisfaction.

Perhaps it is not only the sense of exclusion from the game (in which intellectuals are no longer protected by institutions, or dusty academies, or aesthetic hierarchies; in which all that's left is the struggle for bare survival in the marketplace), but also the authentic need for commitment on the side of good, that has driven intellectuals to accept what is offered them. And what they are offered is a short life in the media: television, newspaper, radio statements, the occasional panel discussion here, an occasional TV forum there.

Intellectuals are not political analysts, they have not had that training, but then again not many political analysts have had any training either. Intellectuals are not military or state strategists, although they not infrequently aspire to be, but then again military strategists are often former pizzeria owners (like the late Croatian Minister of Defense), and state strategists, in the post-Yugoslav states at least, are just former policemen, criminals, bankers, pseudohistorians, and who knows what else. What the media intend for intellectuals—and the reason they invite them—is for them to perform their traditional roles of elders, moral arbiters, priests, humanists.

Among these intellectuals, there are those who have betrayed moral principles in their private lives but who regain their moral aura through this media involvement. There are those who sincerely believe that their words change the world, save lives, and shift the balance in favor of good. There are those who have profited from the whole thing in their own small ways: the constant circulation of their names in the media is a commercial asset, and they can sell one more book, get one more invitation to a conference, give one more interview.

There are those who love the media, and those whom the media love, and those who are more excited by their own assessments of the events than the events themselves. I know one writer who systematically tapes all his television interviews. "Exactly ten years ago I said that the whole affair would end in Kosovo!" proclaims this writer and generous giver of statements on the war, with an expression of undisguised pleasure on his face.

There are cynics who hold that politics today is open to everyone: if actors, criminals, writers, mobsters, fools, and murderers can become president, then politics itself is no longer a particularly serious discipline. There are secret addicts who seek the thrill of powerful emotions and bloody experiences, and war is certainly the bloodiest. There are political or academic authorities on the region, and they are the most ferocious, because they usually hate the region for which they are responsible but will not let it out of their clutches. Finally, there are intellectuals whose courageous analyses, merciless criticisms, and intelligent and incorruptible positions restore our faith in the irreplaceable role of intellectuals on the public social stage.

One way or another, intellectuals, on the Left and on the Right, inside and outside, for this reason or that, with whatever consequences, have involved themselves in *a real event*. And the war is more than a real event, it is an event overloaded with multiple realities. However, a subtle chemical reaction has taken place in reality, and reality is no longer what it was. It has been irradiated by the media, and as is generally the case with radiation, the damage becomes visible only when it is already too late.

2.

In the American town of Littleton, Colorado, at the end of April 1999, during the NATO bombing of Yugoslavia, two schoolboys shot fifteen of their schoolmates. Commenting on the reactions of their fellow citizens who came to lay flowers at the school, one teenage boy on the verge of tears said, "I couldn't believe it. It was better than on MTV."

The human malice which is attributed to people in the Balkans, and which has been fixed forever in the proverbial curse: "May my next-door neighbor's cow die," is expressed differently today: "May you see your house on CNN!"

It is not only reality that has been contaminated by the media but also the immediate victims of that reality. A photograph of captives in the Manjača camp, where the Serbs mistreated Bosnian Muslims, was at one point on the front pages of newspapers all over the world. A tall, exceptionally thin man standing behind barbed wire. Some years later a journalist found the man in Denmark, in a refugee camp, and interviewed him. He had put on about sixty pounds, and was no longer the same man. He went on to complain that he had been exploited and cheated, that his photograph had gone all around the world but he had gotten *nothing* for it. Other people made money from him, selling that picture everywhere. The photograph, a substitute for reality, became the poor man's only identity, but he doesn't match it any more.

The funerals of the children killed in Littleton are only one example of life which has become a movie, or a movie which is life itself. The dead sixteen-year olds had TV biographies ready, because they had been video-taped by their parents since birth. The funeral of Rachel Joy Scott, complete with video presentation *(A Celebration of Rachel's Life)*, musical accompaniment *(Why Do These Things Happen?)*, photographs, video-postcards of the Colorado landscape, and the sincere tears of her schoolmates, who wept, raised their eyes to the sky ("I love you, Rachel!"), and at the same time gave astonishingly eloquent funeral speeches in front of the camera ("I don't know how I can do it, but she is with me now to make me strong enough") demonstrated that, televised from birth, they were all acting/living a film in front of the TV cameras. A director's hand was unnecessary: no one spoke out of turn, no one said one word more than was needed, everyone wept at the right time.

An event—and an event is an event once it has been thoroughly aired in the media—becomes a goose which lays golden eggs with the speed of a popcorn machine. The death of Princess Di, the Clinton-Lewinsky affair, the NATO bombing of Yugoslavia, the massacre in Littleton are all events. The event industry works with such power and speed that it is impossible for ordinary observers to establish what is what. They simply participate. Through their participation in an event, the masses confirm its relevance and semantic productivity and prolong its life. Without consumers, an event is not an event.

Through media contamination, a real event is fictionalized (what an old-fashioned word!), for that is the only way it can be consumed, de-realized (deprived of its reality), and hyper-realized (made more real than reality itself). It begins to function the same way as the texts of popular culture do (movies, TV shows, cartoons, trivial literature, celebrities, and so on). Sometimes a real event actually becomes a text of popular culture. In order for this to happen, the text of mass culture must be *producerly;* it must stimulate and produce meanings, bring them into conflict, engage and activate the emotions of the consumers, question but also confirm the fundamental set of values which consumers have. In that sense, not every event has the potential to function as a text of mass culture, just as not every text does either.

In order for a real-life event (Clinton's case, for example) to function as a text of mass culture, it must produce pleasure. The pleasures can be of different kinds: pleasure is produced by the archetypal victory of good over evil, but also by evil itself. Pleasure is produced by trashing the symbols of authority (that is exactly what Monica Lewinsky and Paula Jones did), but also by defending them. Each group must be able to bring to this event its own set of values (American women, African-Americans, Republicans, Democrats, traditional America, white-trash America, and so on). The possibility of free and unhindered involvement in the event also promotes pleasure, as in the *Jerry Springer Show,* where the viewers are at the same time observers and participants, audience and actors, watchers and watched.

Mass culture is also a big business. It is pointless to investigate how much money people have made from an event—souvenir-sellers to publishers, Monica Lewinsky to the journalists and commentators on the Clinton case— and to moralize over the paychecks involved in the business. Everyone knows there's no business like show business.

The final episode of the tragic dissolution of Yugoslavia has the potential to become one such text of mass culture. The division into good and evil is clear at last: evil Serbs vs. good Albanians; evil Milošević vs. good Bill Clinton, who offered five million dollars to whoever would bring Milošević to trial at the Hague Tribunal. The Kosovo war episode polarized consumers into those who were for the bombing and those who were against it (texts of popular culture cannot endure ambivalence). Multiple kinds of pleasure were activated in the consumer: the excitement of learning something new (Kosovo, Albanians, Serbs) and participating directly in world events, the glow of compassion for the terrorized (the Kosovo Albanians), the pride of protecting them, the thrill of fear and horror (rape, corpses' heads, dead bodies, young girls' scalps), the fun of playing (video games, bombardiers, soldiers) with powerful technology (bombs which transform buildings into ruins with laser precision), the satisfaction of subjugating the old, evil world (Serbs, criminals, communists and communist dictatorship, the past) and of affirming the new, good world (democracy, the new world order, technology, the future). Bill Clinton himself, using the rhetoric of a movie review, book proposal, or blurb, described the war like this: "All the ingredients for a major war are there. Ancient grievances, struggling democracies, and, at the center of it all, a dictator in Serbia who has done nothing since the Cold War ended but start new wars and pour gasoline on the flames of ethnic and religious division."

The media, television in particular, transform events into entertainment, simply because entertainment, and not information, has become the main engine of the mass media. Media presentation has reduced American trials (O. J. Simpson) and American political life (the case of Clinton) to mass amusement. Of course, it is precisely as amusement that political life achieves the extreme point of its democracy (or the extreme point of its illusion of democracy). Filtered through the powerful media, American political life has become carnivalized. Everybody is welcome to participate in the carnival: people of all classes and all races.

The media determine many things, including casting. From being an ordinary, not-very-bright civil servant, Paula Jones acquired the media aura of a vulgar American heroine, representative of white-trash America (the most reliable television consumers), and she became for a moment an ironic, subversive symbol of the democratic challenge to another American symbol, the White House. The media select suitable professionals, TV lawyers, journalists, intellectuals, spin doctors, public figures; everyone who knows how to make a media fuss around an event. So the Clinton case produced a large number of media commentators who transformed it into various forms of popular entertainment, turning a political scandal into a Judge Judy-like courtroom show, or wrestling match, or porn movie.

The tragic disintegration of Yugoslavia was extensively covered in the media. Armies marched through former Yugoslavia: armies of journalists, TV reporters, film directors, producers, writers, intellectuals, photographers, or simply adventurers who became writers, reporters, journalists, and photographers. Miles of film and tons of paper were used up. Heaps of documentaries, films, books, photographs were produced, even souvenirs (for instance, the volume *Angels of Sarajevo,* in which angel wings are added to real portraits of Sarajevo children in a crude photomontage). The real human tragedy has been televised, filmed, photographed, retold, and chewed over thousands of times in the mouths of consumers but also in the mouths of the participants themselves.

I believe that intellectuals are considering their positions, their roles, and their commitments at a time when *Homo sapiens* have successfully evolved into *Homo scaenicus* (Man the Entertainer). In their engagement with war, intellectuals occupy themselves with the old questions of morality. Morality is the key word of war rhetoric: both Bill Clinton and Slobodan Milošević, both victims and soldiers, talk about morality. Even the NATO military action was presented in the media as a lesson in morality.

If they have already taken on the preferred role of moral arbiters in the media, intellectuals must reflect on their role. One possible consequence of such a confrontation would be for intellectuals to fully professionalize their status and publicly advertise their fee for moral arbitration. This much for their opinion on Kosovo, that much for their opinion on NATO. Intellectual engagement would be a new function, paid media intervention, with an old-fashioned name. If that happens, their engagement will no longer provoke confusion either among themselves, or among those buying their services, or among the media consumers. Another logical, if awkward, result would be to absolve the Serbian intellectuals who advocated the war, because intellectuals—real and pseudo, good guys and bad guys—are all just carrying out their business, selling their moral convictions in the marketplace.

One American TV journalist, a fierce propagandist for Clinton's removal from power and the author of a book on impeachment, declared, "Unfortunately, I don't know how to sell myself properly. I only charge six thousand dollars, while some of my colleagues get up to twenty thousand."

That is to say, one by-product of the engagement of heaps of American *experts* in the Clinton affair was numerous appearances throughout America. The woman who did not know how to sell herself charged a modest six thousand dollars per appearance. And her appearance was unlikely to have been an academic lecture, but rather the moderation of public discussion about the Clinton case, in other words moderation of gossiping, lasting one or two hours.

Perhaps, therefore, a public gesture of de-heroizing the intellectual's media role would be welcome. In that way, the old proverb that *a wise word is worth gold* would come true. And the joke about the mute child could have a different ending: "I'll talk if you buy me a bicycle!" the boy would say.

There is another, romantic choice, which would suit the traditional role of the humanist better. The author of every written or spoken word about war, of every book and every public appearance, could forego his fee, or ask that the fee be directed to those places which he was pronouncing judgment on, fighting for, or representing. The author would then have to forego publishing his photograph on book jackets or in newspapers, in order to avoid self-promotion. The authors of books about war crimes, rape, or atrocities would not only have to pay a tax for every untruth, inexact detail, and inaccurate figure, but also ask that every penny earned from their books go toward some children's kindergarten or school library in Kosovo or wherever.

Only in this way could a clearer border be established between authentic commitment and paid intellectual amusement under the label of commitment. Many of my fellow writers will ask: Why from us? Why from the most innocent, why from *humanists?* Because a moral tax should be levied on those who take on a moral role. So from humanists above all.

There is a third choice, the one most likely to become actual intellectual-media practice. The media, especially television, will produce so-called media intellectuals, with the task of thinking about the world. Since not all intellectuals are *media-compatible*, the services of the chosen ones will be well paid. A media intellectual will be paid for promoting the illusion that we, ordinary people, think about this or that issue the same way he, the clever one, thinks. Or for promoting the equally satisfying illusion that we think the opposite. The media intellectual will have to accept the consequences of media engagement, namely that it is not the message that matters, but the messenger. The intellectual will settle for life in the media orbit with his equals, fellow messengers, "celebs." The media intellectual will become a celeb, a person without substance or rather of changeable substance, a person to whom media consumers attribute meaning. Just like Monica Lewinsky, whether we are for her or against her. So, for instance, we might get a TV spot of Monica Lewinsky talking warmly with Kosovo refugees. Which is certainly not terrible. What is depressing is only the great likelihood that her moral message would have far greater significance than the intellectual's.

And what about me, where do I belong? It is hard to say: I am both inside and outside, both local and foreign. With the money I make from this essay I plan to buy a pair of shoes, Louis Vuitton or Gucci. And I won't think twice; that is how brazen I've become. That's how much I get. I would ask for more but my media rating is low, they say.

1999

Having Fun

To talk about kitsch became impolite at the very moment when the world itself was turning kitsch. Notice that Kafka writes about the bureaucracy at times when the bureaucracy is still almost an innocent creature. Later on, when it swallowed our lives, it became self-evident and thus invisible.... The point I want to make is this: the only time when one can recognize a phenomenon in all its horror is when it is still new.—Milan Kundera

The "box" is a metaphor!

Recently, as a member of an elite intellectual crew, I found myself in front of TV cameras. Some twenty intellectuals from various countries—scholars, historians of culture, painters, writers, philosophers, university professors, freelance thinkers—had been invited to discuss beauty. The host of the program was unusual, like the program itself. We had five hours for our discussion and could take even longer if we wanted. The guests who were used to TV cameras were in their element, others were more restrained, but everyone had some experience of the media.

At first I felt uncomfortable, that I had ended up in this group of people by mistake. It turned out that I was indeed a mistake: in the course of the five-hour discussion, I did not say one single word. I was among people I could only have dreamed of being in the same room with, and I was unable to open my mouth. One other participant was silent as a statue, and several only managed to produce half a sentence or so, but these facts were of small comfort.

What happened? The presenter rarely posed a question to an individual, the questions were directed to us all, so the media space was naturally filled by the more spontaneous of us. One writer launched into a monologue about her own depression, although the topic of the discussion was barely connected with depression. A well-known writer fell into the rhetoric of a fighter for human rights, expressing his personal anxiety about events from Uganda to Bosnia. A well-known zoologist joined in and expressed her concern for threatened gorillas. A well-known feminist-oriented humanist talked about herself, even though the discussion seemed to be about something else. Someone used soccer as a metaphor for something, so others defended soccer, thinking that mass entertainment was under attack. A writer began to explain why she was most concerned about children who suffered from attention-deficit disorders. Someone else gathered that this was an attack on the Internet, and a lively defense of life in cyberspace ensued. The well-known humanist—who by this time had taken a mirror out of her handbag in order to fix her lipstick—repeated something about rights and morals. The well-known zoologist—who had taken a stuffed toy monkey eating a stuffed banana out of her bag and placed it in front of her—repeated her concern for the global environment. Three of them immediately rushed in to confess that they believed in God, although their gods were different.

No one is immune

In short, we all found ourselves in an uncommon situation and reacted as best we could. Some spoke out of awkwardness, others were silent out of awkwardness. Some spoke out of politeness; after all, that is why they had been invited. Those who were silent had nothing to say—I could have interpreted the whole episode like that and then simply forgotten it. But that's not what I think. The episode was certainly a slap in the face of my ego, but my disappointment was deeper.

The intellectuals, who had been given full freedom for intellectual discourse—and intellectual discourse, let us remember, "remains one of the most authentic forms of resistance to manipulation and a vital affirmation of the freedom of thought," as Pierre Bourdieu writes in his book *On Television*—

missed their opportunity. They had the chance to dominate the medium, but the medium of TV, Bourdieu's "space for narcissistic exhibitionism," dominated them instead. Within the group itself, relations of power were immediately established: the *fast thinkers* (Bourdieu's term) spoke and the slower ones tried to catch their breath. The former created "a field of forces, a force field," which "contains people who dominate and others who are dominated." Having secured the space, the fast thinkers continued to talk about trivial matters, using the rhetoric of discoverers. Those who did not want to adapt, or could not adapt, to the tone and topics which had been imposed remained silent.

Knowing that I came from the former Yugoslavia, for example, the well-known writer anxious about Uganda and Bosnia could have generously permitted me to pick up some crumbs and say what was expected of me, a few words about the war in former Yugoslavia which would have confirmed that he was right. However, his passion to present himself was stronger. "People are ready to do almost anything to be the first to see and present something. The result is that everyone copies each other in the attempt to get ahead; everyone ends up doing the same thing. The search for exclusivity, which elsewhere leads to originality and singularity, here yields uniformity and banality," writes Bourdieu.

What does an intellectual need to become a star?

After the first part of our TV-marathon, one of the members of our intellectual crew made a funny graph: he accurately identified the fast thinkers and calculated the frequency of reaction by person. He identified the subgroups which formed among the fast thinkers in the course of the discussion, and their real or false confrontations. I had also been amusing myself with calculations. (What else can an incompatible member of a group do but find satisfaction in an arrogant analysis of the compatible?) It turned out that the fast thinkers among us were media stars. The stars were, in fact, aggressive, but on-screen this aggression was transformed into an impression of sincerity, interest in the subject, a high degree of socialization, and a generally positive image. I was troubled by the question of whether or not one can calculate the qualities that make a thinking person a star.

Banality is the mother of all wisdom

Fast thinkers are intellectuals who follow the rules of the media. That was what the majority of the participants in our television program did, although in fact, for once, they did not need to: the program was set up according to their wishes and they could do whatever they wanted to do.

Accepting the fundamental assumption that television is the most democratic medium means being prepared to speak simplified sentences about everything, with feigned or genuine naturalness; in other words, to produce banality. The production of banality can be interpreted as a form of kindness towards the imagined mass viewer, but also as an expression of arrogance (the mass viewer is stupid, this is all he can understand). The production of banality presumes that the viewer enjoys watching clever people on television saying things that they could say themselves, not offending in any way the self-respect of the imagined majority consumer. Bourdieu again: "Whether you are talking about a speech, a book, or a message on television, the major question of communication is whether the conditions for reception have been fulfilled: does the person who's listening have the tools to decode what I'm saying? When you transmit a 'received idea' it's as if everything is set, and the problem solves itself. Communication is instantaneous because, in a sense, it has not occurred; or it only seems to have taken place. The exchange of commonplaces is communication with no content other than the fact of communication itself."

If the world of triviality steals the language of erudition in the name of its own legitimization in the marketplace (so, for instance, an ordinary clothes shop in New York is called "The Philosophy of Fashion," and a science-fiction TV show about morphs does not fail to mention Kafka), then it is also true that intellectuals themselves do little to protect their field. On the contrary, both sides support each other. The market intellectualizes triviality, intellectuals trivialize intellectuality. Why do intellectuals do this? So as not to be accused of being conceited, of speaking a language no one can understand? In order to pander to the imagined mass consumer? Or simply because the medium determines the message?

The intellectuals in this TV program did not, in the end, think; they performed the act of thinking, their capacity for thinking about everything. At the same time, they did not avoid the tropes of mass culture, but on the contrary affirmed them (depression, the polluted environment, moral responsibility, and so forth). Consciously or unconsciously, the intellectuals performed intellectual kitsch, which they could, of course, have easily defended: it is absurd to speak on television in a language which no one outside the chosen few understands, isn't it?

Simplification has become a kind of unwritten rule of public discourse, the *lingua franca* of public opinion. The retelling (a refined word for gossip) of philosophy instead of philosophizing, the imitation of literature instead of literature, gossip about culture instead of culture itself, the politically correct retelling of political subjects instead of real political opinions—this has all permeated public life, as Kundera described in the quotation in my epigraph.

We live in a time of ever more successfully infantilizing the cultural zone which thirty years ago was still called "high culture." Judging by the bestseller lists, inauthentic books do better than authentic ones, and the bestseller lists themselves are no longer information about the literary stock market but an institution for legitimizing literary and intellectual values. The book versions of the movie versions of literary works sell far better than the literary works themselves.

All of us who found ourselves in front of the TV cameras in the episode I've been describing were manipulating and manipulated, victors and losers, authentic and inauthentic, responsible for the overturning of values which took place there but also its victims. We could compare this to mothers who alter their language and babble when they talk to their children. But in this case, if they do it too long they might forget the language of adults. Which is not so terrible if no one remembers what adult language is supposed to sound like any more.

Hip

In the American academic magazine *Lingua Franca* (November 1998), there was a cheerful article called "Advertisements for Myself," about the web pages of certain American university professors. It turns out that, in the struggle for popularity, some professors demonstrate that good taste is not their strong point (to use hopelessly old-fashioned language). On these web pages you can find pictures of the professors (sometimes in their swimsuits!), details from their private lives, short confessions about their sexual, religious, or culinary preferences, and other juicy bits of information. As I read the article, I got stuck on the description of the web page of a professor I know personally. She had decorated her web page with photographs of herself massaging the tired shoulders of her students and reading their tarot cards. She listed these two things among her favorite social activities.

To be an intellectual today means above all to be a conformist, to adapt to the alleged laws of the market. Not even academic intellectuals are protected from the laws of the market, especially not American ones. They can easily end up without a job, but can also, attracted by unusually high salaries, join a different university team, just like football stars. The image of the intellectual today no longer corresponds to the old-fashioned idea about the individual defending "freedom of thought." The intellectual today is a socialite who adapts to political, cultural, and intellectual mainstream trends and represents what is expected of every decent thinking person. If he shocks, he does so not through his opinions but by publishing naked photographs of himself in the tabloids, which was what one well-known French fast thinker did for lack of any better photo opportunity (the shelling of Sarajevo had already happened).

Today's intellectual has to be *hip, cool, mega,* which in practice means frequently making references to mainstream mass culture, being mildly radical (i.e., performing false radicalism), being mildly subversive (i.e., performing false subversiveness), being an intellectual entertainer. "The problem is not that academics have abandoned their sacred high-culture responsibilities for a changer and night in the disco, but that in so doing they have uncritically reaffirmed the mass media's favorite image about itself," writes Thomas Frank in *The Baffler.*

Are we having fun yet?

A recent article in *Time* magazine was called "Readers Wonder: Are We Having Any Fun Yet?" It claims that contemporary German literature is boring, so Germans devour American literature, which is not boring. "German postwar literature suffers from fun-and-entertainment prohibition, the taboo-ization of many topics, and a great melancholy," was the way it was described for *Time* by Dietrich Schwanitz, a best-selling German writer and teacher of English literature at the university of Hamburg. "Everyone in Germany wants to write like Franz Kafka or Samuel Beckett," he explained. Stefan Bauer, the editor of *Gong* magazine, says that the writers who are considered artists in Germany today write "incomprehensible highbrow fiction."

To be an intellectual today means above all to be boring. Both of the Germans quoted, who condemn contemporary German literature, use a typical repertoire of accusations: *highbrow, incomprehensible, melancholy, no fun.* And the remark about taboo-ization is typical as well. Mass culture—whether it is a matter of jeans, MTV, Coca-Cola, a movie, a music video, or a book—always uses the same self-promotional myth: it, mass culture, breaks taboos, it is unconventional, fresh, avant-garde, subversive, impudent, and never, never boring. None of which, of course, is true.

Writers who accuse German literature of being boring, using commonplaces so common that the reader is saddened to read them, are young people, I imagine. To be young is a guarantee of *subversiveness, authenticity, unconventionality, fun!* In practice, to be young is the surest guarantee that you and your whole self-promotional package will be catapulted into the happy, hectic, and financially rewarding paths of mainstream culture.

Fun-loving culture

Brotherhood on earth will be achieved through kitsch, said Milan Kundera. It has long since been achieved. There is no great difference between a Lisbon fishmonger in Alfama and the barmaids in the little bars on each floor of the Hotel Oktjabrskaja in St. Petersburg. They both watch the same American and Mexican soap operas on TV. Only the word "kitsch," the object of intellectual interest in the sixties, has been squeezed out of circulation. Its place has been taken by the *industry* (film, publishing), *entertainment, pleasure,* and *fun.*

Two years ago I was teaching at an American university. My students did not know what the word "kitsch" meant. During a recent lecture I gave in Germany, a student asked what I had meant by the terms "high literature" and "trivial literature"; I had used them, apologizing for the fact that they were old-fashioned.

"Fun-loving culture"—that is how Neil Postman defined American culture some fifteen years ago in his book *Amusing Ourselves to Death.* Since then, fun-loving culture has taken over the world. The *Washington Post* reported that "international sales of software and entertainment products totaled $60.2 billion in 1996, more than any other U.S. industry, according to Commerce Department data and industry figures. Since 1991, when the collapse of the Soviet Union opened new markets around the world to the United States, total exports of intellectual property from the United States have risen nearly 94 percent in dollar terms, these statistics indicate. And that does not include the untold billions of dollars in revenue lost each year to illegal copying." In the same article, Todd Gitlin affirms that American popular culture is "the latest in a long succession of bidders for global unification. It succeeds the Latin imposed by the Roman Empire and the Catholic Church and Marxist Leninism imposed by Communist governments."

As I am writing these lines, millions of people in 52 countries around the world are watching the teenage TV series *Buffy the Vampire Slayer,* young Vietnamese are entertaining themselves listening to American music in a restaurant chain called "Apocalypse Now," Iranians are going wild about *Titanic, Baywatch* is watched from South America to China, Oprah Winfrey unites a loyal female audience all over the world, and Jerry Springer has become an icon of the Springerization of all aspects of public life: politics, culture, journalism, television.

Only the "fundamentalists" watch nothing. And no one except them wants to be excluded from the global brotherhood. Our golden consumer age bases its profits on the universal desire to belong to the global brotherhood.

The train is also a metaphor

In the summer of 2000, I traveled in a train. It carried about a hundred writers, most of them young, from dozens of European countries. We traveled for a month and a half, from the south of Europe to the north of Europe. A hundred writers is not much, but it is nevertheless some kind of sample of one part of the human population engaged in the activity called literature. We traveled through different European environments, some of which were "problematic." Twenty years ago, a hundred writers would have leapt up to write some kind of petition, make some public statement, some kind of protest. In our train there were no activities of that kind. At the end of the trip, I admit, the writers wrote a tepid statement, but it was about the practical side of the writer's job (a demand that the European Union ensure more money for translation from small languages into other small languages). These writers were apparently satisfied with their cultural niche: their states, nations, the European Union, Europe, literature. We passed through twelve countries and there were Belorussians and Russians and Lithuanians, Cypriots, Turks and Greeks, Serbs and Croats among us. But few seemed to show any interest in politics, in reflections about Europe or the investigation of the concept of literature itself. What brought the writers to life were words such as *lobby, network, cultural management.*

Eco's typology of apocalyptic and integrated intellectuals *(apocalittici e integrati)* is out-of-date. Almost everyone is integrated. The apocalyptic, the melancholic, the tedious, the elitists are rare birds in the cultural scene today. To take them on and confront them—which, in the absence of enemies, representatives of mass culture are still glad to do—is just as absurd as it would be for some Texas senator today to make a campaign speech about battling communism.

"What Orwell feared were those who would ban books. What Huxley feared was that there would be no reason to ban a book, for there would be no one who wanted to read one. Orwell feared those who would deprive us of information. Huxley feared those who would give us so much that we would be reduced to passivity and egoism. Orwell feared that the truth would be concealed from us. Huxley feared the truth would be drowned in a sea of irrelevance. Orwell feared we would become a captive culture. Huxley feared we would become a trivial culture, preoccupied with some equivalent of the feelies, the orgy porgy and the centrifugal bumblepuppy. In short, Orwell feared that what we hate will ruin us, Huxley feared that what we love will ruin us," wrote the apocalyptic Neil Postman, adding that Huxley was right.

As far as I am concerned, I was neither integrated nor apocalyptic until now. I was a hybrid, *intecalyptic*. Now I'm integrated. I have accepted Kundera's advice that it is impolite to talk about omnipresent things. I have decided to join the global brotherhood, which perhaps I was a member of all along, only I didn't want to admit it. It is true that I have no alternative. Obedient integration into the global brotherhood fills me with an almost metaphysical joy. *So, are we having any fun yet?*

We sure are.

2000

6 — Well, Goodbye

Well, good-bye. And thank you for happening to pass me.

House Spirits

There is more than one way to burn a book.—Ray Bradbury

Let us look carefully at these photographs. Both were taken on May 1, 1949, at the May Day parade in Belgrade. I was a baby, forty-five days old.

In the first picture, behind the first row of girls, there is a banner which reads *Long Live the Federal People's Republic of Yugoslavia, a Land of Freedom, Democracy and Progress!* On the right side of the photograph there is an elbow, in all likelihood a policeman's. The young men and women in the parade accompany gigantic books on wheels. On the spine of the horizontal book it says: *Books for the People.* Let us look further. On the book with open pages it says: *Onward into the Battle for the Realization of the Five-Year Plan for Building an Independent and Happy Yugoslavia.* The open book is resting on the spine of another book whose title cannot be seen. But the letter "S" in the top line and the letters "TAL" in the second line suggest that it is *Capital* by Karl Marx (spelled "Marks" in Slavic languages). It is 1949. Yugoslavia is in the middle of a serious conflict with the Soviet Union and all the countries of the Warsaw Pact. That is why the book is leaning on Marx's *Capital,* not on some work of Lenin's or a portrait of Stalin.

Now the second photograph. Four books are piled in a pyramid, on top of which sits a triangle with a star in the center (the triangle with the star suggests the partisan cap, the *titovka*). On the lowest book, turned towards the camera, it says: *Our Five-Year Publishing Plan*. On the spine of the same book, it says *Textbooks*. On top of the textbooks lies *Literature,* on top of that *Science,* and on top of that *Children's Books*. Underneath the titles of the books are numbers which can barely be made out. Perhaps the numbers of published volumes. From the thickness and size of the books, it seems that textbooks will play the most important role in the coming five-year plan. On the second book we can see a blackened rectangle which in the photograph looks like a censor's mark. But it is an opening in the vehicle cab, and inside is the invisible face of the driver. On the third book from the bottom is written *Education (Prosveta)*. This was the name of one of the largest Yugoslav publishing companies.

These photographs of a May Day parade were taken when I was a baby, a month and a half old. The parades I saw later, on television, looked different. Then, after a while, the May Day parades disappeared. Of the rich repertoire of communist spectacles, the longest to endure was Tito's birthday. In fact, spectacles died with Tito. Although one or two celebrations of his birthday were held even after his death, under the slogan of the day: *Even after Tito—Tito.*

Books for the people!

Books for the people! Culture for the people! These were two early communist slogans, under whose robust ideological wing the program of spreading literacy, educating the masses, and democratizing culture was carried out. Even today, I sometimes hear the phantom echo of communist legends about cheery grannies who learned to read in their nineties, or unstoppable blind people who became scientists and champion slalom skiers.

Even the day of my birth was marked with a book. When my father visited my mother in the hospital, he brought her a book as a present, which he bought because of its appropriate title: Maxim Gorky's *Mother.*

In my childhood I was fed communist myths about poor village children who later invented electricity, like Nikola Tesla, or who later beat the fascists and became political leaders who could speak ten languages fluently and play the piano, like Tito. My textbooks bristled with slogans like *In work is salvation, Knowledge is power,* and *Books are our best friends.* My school teachers convinced me that knowledge and art were the two human activities that deserved the greatest respect.

Yugoslav early-communist life was filled with rich *artistic-educational activities.* Even the smallest town had its House of Culture, which contained cinemas, amateur theaters, and libraries. Every village had its amateur theater. Amateurism (amateur filmmakers, amateur actors, amateur photographers, amateur poets) democratized culture in a predominantly peasant country, which Yugoslavia was before the Second World War. *Hamlet* was performed by half-literate workers and farmers, but as a result, people whose lives did not destine them for such things were familiar with the names Shakespeare and Hamlet. With the coming of television into the home, amateurism gradually disappeared, and with it the Workers' Universities and Houses of Culture.

I love to watch the Oprah Winfrey show. Learning, self-education, the achievement of high personal goals, *a healthy soul in a healthy body,* support for the poor *(Universities for the Poor!),* support for the young and the talented, support for the education of adults, the belief that a healthy individual leads to a healthy society, the belief that the written word can change lives (and the world!), and that *knowledge is power*—all of these are commonplaces of early communist cultural propaganda. It sometimes seems to me that Oprah is my primary-school teacher, appearing to me through my TV screen after all these years. She may have changed her language, her skin color, and her appearance, but I understand and love everything that she says because I heard it all a long time ago.

The democratization of culture in capitalist societies has been brought about by the market and expanded by globalization. The democratization of culture in most communist societies came in a package with communism.

Let us return to the photographs. They were taken in 1949, at the time of the break with the Soviet bloc. Just four years later, Yugoslav writers officially broke with socialist realism. In the same year, 1953, Yugoslav cinemas showed their first Hollywood film, *Water Ballet,* starring Esther Williams. After that, the doors were wide open for Hollywood films. And they fit extraordinarily well into the culture of that time. Let's be honest, there is no essential difference between the aesthetics of Esther Williams films and the aesthetics of the communist spectacles. Except that Esther Williams puts on a better show. But America was a big, rich country, untouched by war, and Yugoslavia was small, poor, and war-torn.

Summoning the devil

The word "goodbye" is not one of my favorite words. When I was young, I believed in the meaning of words. There is a custom in old Russian folklore: when people leave a house where they have lived, they leave slippers in front of the fire so that the house spirits, *domovye,* can follow them. In popular belief, the house spirits are the keepers of memory and continuity. I myself have been known, in places where I had to say *goodbye* but was afraid of the definitiveness of the word, to leave something behind me as a pledge of my return. It was a symbolic act of subverting the meaning of the word and that little subversion was simply a proof of my belief in the power of words. Today I cannot even remember how many things I have left in other people's apartments, including slippers. Nomads know it is cheaper to leave things behind than to take them along.

Goodbye until the Next War! was the title of a Yugoslav movie from about twenty years ago. Artists often blurt out all kinds of nonsense. But it turns out that some of it comes to pass. The title of the film came true: Yugoslavs really did meet each other in a new war.

In primitive cultures there is a fear of words, a fear that their meanings will come to life. *Chertyhanie* is a Russian word which can be translated as *summoning the devil.* Many of my fellow countrymen, Yugoslav writers and intellectuals, repeated the word *war* until the devil was summoned and war actually appeared.

Book burners

How the citizens of Yugoslavia said *goodbye* to their country was very harsh. Their country, lives, houses, books, documents, photographs, biographies, maps, language, schools, things, memories, libraries—everything disappeared.

In Sarajevo the National Library was destroyed, hundreds of thousands of books transformed into ash. The books which the Serbs didn't manage to destroy with their shells were destroyed by the citizens of Sarajevo themselves—for fuel. First they used so-called communist briquettes, the collected works of communist thinkers. It was their calorific value that the inhabitants of Sarajevo most prized. When such volumes are wrapped in wire they burn slowly, like coal, the Sarajevans claim. Shakespeare himself served as fuel too; in the struggle for survival, neither ideological nor aesthetic priorities matter.

In Croatia, at the same time, the new nationalist government quietly supported the cleansing of unsuitable books from the libraries: books that were *Serbian, communist, Cyrillic, anti-Croatian, anti-fascist,* and others (including, again, books by Shakespeare). The book burners did not much care for distinctions. Thousands of books ended up in the trash. Dead and living writers were erased from school curricula, from libraries, from literary history and literary life. The work was carried out by intellectuals, *executioners,* volunteers.

Manuscripts do not burn: one day everything will return to its proper place, history cannot be erased, new libraries will be built, new books will be printed; so the cultural optimists console us. Optimists are not usually familiar with the practice of destroying; they look on things from a blessedly distanced "historical" perspective, hence their optimism. In fact, it is hard to replace destroyed books. For a long time, there will be no money for such things. The mafia governments have robbed their own people and plunged them into debt for many years to come. If there ever is any money, it is hard to imagine that books will be a priority, just as it is hard to imagine that literature itself will have the same meaning that it had at the time of its destruction. Later revisions of cultural history are usually of interest to merely a small circle of experts.

October cookies and Campbell's Soup

Communism's farewell in Eastern Europe was not only a farewell to a system but to a whole culture. It was a dual culture: a culture of supporting the system and a culture of resisting the system, a culture of promoting the system but also a culture of subverting it. The culture of resistance developed rich art forms and trends, such as "soc-art," whose main task was to describe and defamiliarize the Soviet ideological world, from Stalinist camps to October cookies. Today, resistance culture has been replaced by instant culture. Soviet, Hungarian, Czech, Yugoslav, Polish, and Romanian films have disappeared. Writers, as well as their place in the social hierarchy, have been shoved to the margins. Many artists ended up in exile, and only a few returned. A whole culture vanished before it managed to be properly reevaluated. In radical political changes, like the collapse of communism, you don't think about what is worth saving and bringing along. In Lithuania and Estonia, for instance, the occasional Cyrillic letter has managed to survive only in places where it was impossible to destroy it: on manhole covers!

They say that October cookies no longer exist. Campbell's Soup, the icon of modern culture, sits on American supermarket shelves. Millions of Americans slurp that soup, and its famous iconographer, Andy Warhol, hangs in American museums. Everything is as it should be. Except now you can also buy Campbell's Soup in Moscow supermarkets. With the soup, the Russians slurp the symbolic dawning of a new life and connection to the "normal world." Soup is an effective balm for a lengthy trauma, but at the same time also its confirmation.

Traumas

I don't know how other postcommunist people or places relate to their cultural past, but I know that former Yugoslavs did not leave slippers by the

fire in order that their house spirits—a pledge of memory and continuity—
should follow them. Instead, they say that their house was small and hate-
ful, they could hardly wait to destroy it and start life over again.

In destroying their shared home, the post-Yugoslav states waged a fierce
battle on two parallel fronts. On one front, memory was destroyed: a battle
was waged, real and mental, against everything *Yugoslav.* On the other front,
national ideologues embarked on the production of national phantasms. National culture was reduced to representing a hazy national identity and confirming these phantasms.

All in all, the participants in the post-Yugoslav national cultures found
themselves in ruins which they had themselves created. Finding themselves
in a position of threefold trauma (the stigma of communism, the collapse of
Yugoslavia and war, and the newly composed national culture)—in other
words, finding themselves in a triply inauthentic role—writers, artists and
intellectuals refuse to confront their own trauma. Incapable of confronting
the past in which they grew up and the reasons for the deconstruction of
their lives, they obediently accept the identities imposed on them and per-
petuate the language of inauthenticity. Unprepared to confront these changes,
they adapt to their new situation as though nothing had happened.

I recently traveled through Eastern Europe with a group of writers. At a
small border crossing between Poland and Russia, we were met with bread
and salt by the chief of the local police, the manager of the station, a local
schoolteacher who made a welcoming speech, and a women's amateur folk
group. With glittering golden crowns on their teeth, the women sang and
danced the way they always had.

In the railroad station in Vilnius, we met with a different reception. In
the station hall was a podium where a jazz band was playing, while poets
recited to us from raised lecterns in the corners: a Chinese poet in Chinese,
an American in English, a Lithuanian in Lithuanian, and a Russian in
Russian. Everything happened simultaneously: the poets recited, each for
himself, the jazz band played. This cacophonic performance was *art* produced by the traumatized imagination of its East European author. It was
a product of new agitprop. The performance had a hidden message: we,

Lithuanians, are West Europeans, we have nothing in common with (Russian) communist culture, we are a cosmopolitan, multicultural society like the rest of civilized Western Europe, we don't bore our guests by thumping folklore at you, we don't stick bread and salt into your mouths, we are "normal." A little later I learned from a Lithuanian guidebook that Vilnius is the "geographical center of Europe" (whatever that means), that the Pope's mother was Lithuanian, and that the Nazis (whose?) did indeed behave badly towards the local Jews, but that the Lithuanians themselves barely survived the heavy Russo-communist repression.

I was to come across this language of trauma (we are victims!) again in Riga, in Tallin, in St. Petersburg, in conversation with a Bulgarian poet ("I am ashamed of being Bulgarian. I would like to be someone else," he said), in Minsk. I recognized this language because I had already learned it in Ljubljana, Zagreb, Belgrade, Skopje.

I was to experience a certain relief in Moscow, wandering among the street stalls with souvenirs. There, on the stalls, I came across market tolerance. I saw traditional lacquered boxes with new motifs from the life of the "New Russians" (mafiosi in Mercedes, with tennis rackets in their hands, surrounded by Russian Barbies), t-shirts with Stalin's portrait and hard-core communist slogans, cups with reproductions of Malevich's signature, Soviet military caps eaten by moths, and *matryoshka* dolls in the form of Russian writers: in Pushkin is a smaller doll of Tolstoy, in Tolstoy Dostoyevsky, in Dostoyevsky Chekhov, in Chekhov Gogol.

Convalescence had begun in the flea market. In the marketplace. Where, they say, it always begins. But I'm not sure culture can be revived by the mere sale of cultural souvenirs, whoever created them: young artists playing with a past which is not theirs or old ones reevaluating their own past. If an authentic language of culture does appear, and I am sure it will, it will come from other sources. One source will be nostalgia. It will appear at a moment of full inner freedom, when the tenant—whether he moved of his own accord or someone else's—leaves slippers by the fire so that the house spirits can follow him.

2000

Questions to an Answer

Mantra

"Globalization" is the current global mantra. The term travels the world like a foreign suitcase, stuck all over with various semantic labels, overloaded with meanings and informed by ideological coloring. Intellectuals called on to consider the meaning and content of the concept fall easily and often into semantic traps. The reason lies in part in the very nature of vogue words, for "the more experiences they pretend to make transparent, the more they themselves become opaque" (Zygmunt Bauman, *Globalization*). Another reason is the concept's heavy ideological baggage, and a third is the breadth of the content it covers, from economics to ecology, from technology and communication to the status of the state, from culture and the media to geopolitics, from the structure of multinationals to the reinterpretation of national identity, from philosophy and an understanding of space and speed to sociology and global migrations. All of these aspects are interconnected, and it is hard to speak about one without taking account of another, or to mention another without considering a third.

Seen from the outside, globalization resembles a rainbow smokescreen through which the face of the Dalai Lama smiles and his voice rings out saying that there can never be enough differently colored flowers.

The global citizen

Who is this global citizen? He is quick, efficient and rational, he is master of his body, technology, and information, he knows who he is and what he wants, and what he wants he buys. He is a highly conscious consumer, who lunches on Japanese sushi and dines on Hungarian goulash. He is flexible, he loves his work, he is highly professional. He is mobile, penetrating, and precise as a bullet. He is a handyman who fixes the world and carries with him the idea of progress. This seductive image of our ideal contemporary, this realization of the myth of Superman, travels globally: New York businessmen and Australian aborigines can identify with this image equally on the TV screen.

In real life (if such a thing exists), things look rather different. If he belongs to the rich part of humanity, a mere third of the total, our contemporary is hardly in a position to understand the logic of the electricity bill he pays, let alone himself and his place in the world. His own daily life is increasingly virtual. The power he possesses is virtual ("The power of virtual is a virtual power," writes Jean Baudrillard in *Paroxysm*), and the reality of the coordinates that determined him until recently (job, class, ethnicity, race, religious affiliation, culture) increasingly escapes him. In the rich choice of "identities" available in the marketplace of identity he can certainly find something to his taste: from the traditional "Blut und Boden" package to sophisticated bisexuality. Unlike yesterday's psychoanalysts, today's contemporary coaches—from "fathers of the nation" and "spiritual gurus" to fashion designers and plastic surgeons—no longer explain who we are, because what does that matter in the virtual world? They tell us what we might become.

If he belongs to the other two thirds of the population of the earth, our contemporary is hungry or "merely" poor. The two worlds, the rich and the poor, live separately. "The riches are global, the misery is local—but there is no causal link between the two," writes Bauman. Statistics reinforce this division between the two worlds: at this moment there are apparently 358 billionaires whose income is equal to the income of 2.3 billion people.

Ideology

The ideology of globalization is just as attractive as the idealized global citizen. Globalization is above all a synonym for the modern age in which work has finally become pleasure, as though we had stumbled into communism.

The ideology of globalization has succeeded in linking and harmonizing two opposing ideas: universalization, and therefore a necessary standardization, and on the other hand the unassailable right to individuality and difference. The globalist ideology which we absorb every day on TV confirms this harmony through pictures of Indian women in saris confidently surfing the Net, or Arab women veiled from head to toe with cell phones ringing under their robes.

The spectacle of globalization is adorned with the old revolutionary ideas of liberty, equality, fraternity, only this time in a world without frontiers. From a practical point of view, globalization is a kind of magic trick. For only magic can help this supposed world without frontiers *annul* and at the same time *maintain* state, national, ethnic, religious, racial, geographic, and other boundaries.

While the ideology is soft, the practice is hard. The practice of the world without frontiers is encountered daily by the millions of people who pour out of "worse" worlds into "better" ones. Apart from the enormous number of migrants who are sent back or die in illegal border crossings, there is also a phantom population of "dead souls," some seventy million people, they say, who circulate like shadows through the "better" worlds with no identity papers.

The designers of the globalization spectacle have at their disposal everything they need: money, media, power, and above all attractive imagery. The skeptics, who ask what's behind the smokescreen, are seen as party poopers, "fundamentalists" who would rather die than quench their thirst with global Coca-Cola. There are no distinctions in such labeling: one finds both Slobodan Milošević and Noam Chomsky in the same category of rejecters of the new world order.

Within the ideological structure of globalization, an allegedly "democratic" media battle is being waged along the lines of this opposition: for progress and the future as opposed to traditionalism, for high technology as opposed to "the plough and the hoe," for global communication as opposed to isolation, for the values of the progressive world as opposed to those of the backward world, for a free market as opposed to poverty, for the peace-loving majority as opposed to the stubborn and warmongering minority. The outcome of the battle is assured in advance.

Culture

Those concerned with culture often fall into the ideological trap produced by the agitprop of globalization. There is a majority who obediently buy into the values of contemporary culture, and a negligible minority who question those values.

Serious criticism of globalization in culture does not come only from the "periphery," from the ranks of the postcolonial, non-Western theoreticians of culture, but also from its "epicenter," the ranks of the American intelligentsia. American critics have no doubt that globalization is another name for American cultural imperialism, Americanization on a global scale. West European intellectuals are far more cautious, because they do not want to be put in the same ideological camp as the Taliban. East European intellectuals are silent: in the traumatized postcommunist states, every form of criticism tends to be labeled "leftist terrorism," which, the opponents claim, favors a return to communism. Besides, "leftists" can easily find themselves in the same basket with local nationalists. "Anti-American" and "anti-European" sentiments serve as a perfect ideological cover for local criminals and people in power: the antiglobalization rhetoric of defending ethnic and cultural difference keeps their territory free of outside control, so that they can continue their criminal activities unmolested.

Intellectuals nowadays concern themselves with the problems of globalization in culture, the problems of its ambivalence, the conjunction of ideology, money, and the market in culture, the question of the future of the book in the electronic age, strategies of media brainwashing and censorship.

They also concern themselves with the organization of media conglomerates, the role of television, the place of educational institutions, the Internet, and the consequences of the domination of American mass culture, which has not only driven high culture (American included) to the margins but has with time lowered even its own standards. It is clear to cultural thinkers that, along with food, the American infotainment industry is America's biggest export, whose expansion can hardly be stopped.

Let us stress here that American "cultural imperialism" does not have a copyright on the strategy itself. At the time of the Soviet bloc, for instance, the system of cultural exchange functioned according to the principle of partial reciprocity—apart from the language, Russian, which was the "official language," just as English is today. There were numerous institutes, translators, and publishers: books circulated widely within the communist bloc. Apart from "high culture" products, there was also the entertainment industry, which was sometimes just a "translation" of American popular culture but was often a successful mixture of pop culture narrative strategies and themes of communist everyday life. In the early 1960s, Yugoslav partisan movies (imitations of American Westerns) had a remarkable penetration through the communist bloc as far as China. Polish, Czech, and Yugoslav TV series made a considerable profit within that not insignificant market. In the pre-American era, in the early 1950s, Mexican and Indian movies were effective popular culture. Before its "Americanization," Yugoslav TV was briefly "Italianized," for instance. Today those former communist markets—from Croatia to China—have been captured by American soap operas, and far cheaper Mexican ones.

What makes the whole issue of globalization more complex today are the dimensions provided by technology. Computer technology is the virtual foundation of globalization, but, who knows, maybe its future grave as well.

Stereotyping

Globalization is in essence a "fundamentalist concept," which has "succeeded in creating a monopoly out of a balanced plurality." Universal, plural language has become the "official language" of globalization (Baudrillard).

In order to bring about communication—and globalization is communication—it is necessary to establish a common language, a system within which the exchange of information functions, or, when we are talking of culture, an exchange and interaction of cultural goods.

To whom, then, are we selling cultural products? Which is the real, but also the mental address to which we send them; who is our favorite addressee? The American cultural industry has secured the global market, and all buyers are welcome, from the Papuans to the Portuguese. Local producers stay at home, placing their goods on local markets or trying to penetrate the American and West European markets. A Polish writer will not exert himself to be published in India; if such a thing does happen, it is just a happy but irrelevant accident. An Indian writer, despite his justified postcolonial bitterness, does not much care whether he is published in some Bulgaria or another. To be published in the Anglo-American market, though—from which the transmission of cultural goods spreads farther afield—means holding in your hand a ticket to the global market lottery.

The other important addressee is the West European market. But importance does not guarantee reciprocity. Despite the fact that his countryman Bertelsmann has bought up half the American publishing industry, a German writer sits in the office of a New York publisher on the same chair and, it seems, with the same prospects of being published as his fellow Russian or Italian writer. Then again, even an American writer with serious literary ambitions has only a slight advantage over the Europeans.

How does the cultural product communicate in the global cultural market?

In souvenir shops in West European cities you can find joke postcards showing stereotypical characteristics of representatives of the European Union countries. These postcards assure us yet again that the English are "cold," the Dutch "stingy," the French "arrogant." These souvenir stereotypes are an innocent joke among equals and will not be taken amiss. That is why, among other things, there are no "colored" French, "Turkified" Germans, "Germanized" Turks, or "Indianized" English among these equals.

The postcards are a message which suggests to the perceptive viewer that the language of unification is a language of stereotyping. The favorite European slogan—"unity through diversity"—treats European "diversity" as a repertoire of cultural stereotypes. It turns out that stereotypes are in fact national and ethnic identity, that it is precisely through stereotypes that the right to difference is realized. But this also means the reverse: that national identity is nothing other than a package of stereotypes.

Stereotyping is the language of politics, television, and mass culture (if it were not so it would not be mass). It is the most effective language of the global cultural market. Thus stereotypes—despite the proclaimed ideology of a world without frontiers, postcolonial theories, the all-uniting Internet, the free exchange of cultural goods—have continued to be the basic formula of communication. For instance, did the Cold War stereotypes disappear with the fall of the Wall or simply change their referents? What happens to the cultural text in a system which promises communication without frontiers but is based on stereotypes? Are stereotypes market labels which sell a product better than anything else, or are they its real content? Are stereotypes not the basic language of every product which communicates globally, including cultural texts themselves?

The global cultural market so rapidly and enthusiastically appropriates the intellectual trends of our time—postcolonialism, feminism, multiculturalism, identity politics—that one sometimes wonders whether the market itself invents intellectual trends in order to make a profit. Today's global cultural bazaar is inundated with products affirming these ideological mantras and transforming them into politically correct kitsch. For example, there's the trend of self-orientalization in literature (and pop music), where artists appear on their book (or CD) covers in semi-oriental outfits like holy prophets of the postcolonial right to difference. Or the cultural products which sprang up in the course of the war in former Yugoslavia, and which contributed to the "balkanization" of the Balkans. Yugoslav filmmakers, pop musicians, artists, and writers reached the global market more easily insofar as their products affirmed the stereotypes of the "wild" and "bloody" Balkans. It is hard to question this kitsch without falling into the corresponding trap of political incorrectness.

Mass culture

The values of mass culture are like the values of the culture of amateurism which flourished under communism and had enormous popular-educational value.

The fundamental assumption of the market is democracy. Everyone is welcome as a consumer, but also as a producer. While the enthusiasm of cultural amateurism under communism was quickly extinguished, giving way to professionalism (whatever that means), the contemporary enthusiasm is not waning because mass culture brings enormous profits.

The market produces perfect globalistic products. The products of mass culture do not destroy stereotypes but confirm and disseminate them. Even with valuable and unique products, the market tries to find appropriate stereotypical packaging. In that sense, a good Japanese film is packaged for the market just as Japanese sushi is. Thus the global market becomes a field for the transmission and expansion of cultural stereotypes. The Japanese mainstream cultural product draws after it the Korean, the Korean the Taiwanese. The cultural menu thus expands, without changing its essence.

For instance, the American television industry abounds in sitcoms intended for numerous groups and subgroups within American society: racial groups (Chinese, Korean, Puerto Rican, Cuban, black), professions (students, doctors, lawyers), social classes, sexual orientations, age groups, genders. Mass culture effectively expands its repertoire with new targeted groups of consumers, but it never abandons its fundamental assumptions: it is "democratic" (accessible to all), it is in one way or another "educational" (for instance, gay sitcoms educate while pacifying the mostly straight audience), and it is "moral," which simply means that it never attacks the basic values (family, religious, ethnic, racial, national).

Global cultural products remind me of the richly illustrated children's encyclopedia which I had as a child, *The World around Us*. The children's encyclopedia was "popular," "educational," and "moral." It often seems to me today that its world has leapt out of its covers and come to life on TV, in the street, in the supermarket, in souvenir shops, in tourist offices. My first instruction in globalization came in my childhood. Today's version, as far as culture is concerned, is equally simplistic.

Local and global

The local/global opposition is one of the most manipulative formulas of the globalistic ideology. The *local* (national, ethnic, regional) implies the right to diversity, as opposed to the *global,* which threatens to iron out those differences. In practice, protected by the ideology of respecting national and ethnic differences, local manipulators often carry out the murky business of local control. For those who do not accept such an interpretation of local and global interconnections, the global becomes the only way out, the field of freedom.

I have experienced the local practice of destroying culture in the name of culture, the practice of destroying monuments and books, the practice of censorship and erasing cultural memory. After such an experience, when it comes to a choice between the *local* and the *global,* I choose the global without a moment's hesitation. Even when "artistic" communication is wrong, deaf, and incomplete (as if it were complete in the "local" environment!), even when it discriminates (as if it doesn't "at home"!), even when it "deprives" me of my right to speak (as if it didn't do that "at home"!), even when my novel might end up being read as a manual for plumbers,[1] despite all that, I choose the global. Even when I hear remarks like the following in an American sitcom: "I wouldn't know. I'll have to ask my cleaning lady, she has a Ph.D., she's Bulgarian. . . ." I hear them often. My fear of the local is stronger than my skepticism of the global. Simply on the basis of my traumatic experience of the local, the global gains additional points, as long as we accept this opposition.

---

[1] In a review of a novel in the *New York Review of Books,* I came across the following description of its narrative strategy: "the narrative pressure of his novel comes and goes in spurts, like water in an Eastern European plumbing system."

Museumification

Culture buffs quite rightly complain that the American film industry has ruined small European cinema production. However, some small European cinema industries ruined themselves even before the American film industry came along.

In Zagreb, for instance, there was a famous school of animated film. Many of its illustrators were famous, and for a while, thanks to the importance of the school, Zagreb was a meeting place for many international artists in the field. It is true that the gradual decline of the school had begun somewhat earlier, but the main blow—ethnic cleansing—was carried out by the rigid, nationalist Croatian cultural milieu at the time of so-called national homogenization. An American producer recently made a series of DVDs about East European animated film and one of them includes films from the Zagreb school. Thanks to computer technology, a small segment of European culture has been preserved. By the Americans.

Thanks to technology, and also to its ideology, globalization has opened up space for the protection, the museumification, and the affirmation of small cultures. Does the museumification of culture mean culture? Even if it is a commercial activity disguised as concern for culture, the result is the same: what was threatened with disappearance has been saved. But in most cases, museumification is not, nor could it be, commercial. A quick visit to Harvard University's Widener Library reveals that the books of the most minor Macedonian, Croatian, Bosnian, and Serbian writers—whose own literary environment already forgot about their existences, whose books can't be found in their local libraries, who may already have forgotten themselves that once upon a time they had written a book or two—the books are there, living an eternal life on safe library shelves. And more than that: they are saved in the original, minor language in which they were written and published.

Turning it off, turning it on

When we deal in concepts such as *art,* we do not call the meaning of the concept into question. However, in our world of shattered perspectives, even art no longer has a self-evident meaning. Postcolonial theories have re-vived the problem of the identity of the Other (Asiatic, African, Albanian, Aboriginal) and its culture, values, and aesthetic canon and standards. The Other demands that his position be reinterpreted, de-stereotyped, decolonized, and given equal rights and power. Demanding a fundamental redefinition of relations between the colonizer and the colonized, the Other assumes that the identity of the colonizer is complete and stable. But that is not quite true anymore either. Today, in the context of the dominance of American mass culture, West European culture—as a firm system of values that has been dominant for centuries—is itself another museum, albeit some-what larger and fuller than a museum of Indian crafts or African masks.

So what has become of art itself? The West European canons, destroyed several decades ago, have never been revived. Duchamp's ironic destructive gesture has been perpetuating itself in one form or another for decades, and its message does not change. Are we certain that in this new context—of shattered perspectives, different cultural identities, and consequently the dif-ferent status and function of art in the world of the global market—we know what we are talking about when we use the word "art"? Or are we sticking an old label onto a new product?

The contemporary colonizer is the market. The market vacuums up every resistance, takes into account every criticism and even anticipates it, turning it to its own profit. The market colonizes us without our being aware of it and does so with our own values, whether they are called iden-tity, ethnicity, the right to difference, or anything else. It is hard to imagine effective resistance to money, media potentates, conglomerates, the mo-nopoly of distribution chains, or "market fundamentalism" as such.

The "money against money" strategy can restore the destroyed balance, but the question remains as to which "culture" the benefactors will favor. European cultural bureaucracy often spares no expense when it is a matter of a "representative" culture or the culture of representation (the idea of Europeanness, European cultural standards, the defense of regional cultures and languages, and so on). Institutions, festivals and conferences, funds and foundations, NGOs and cultural managers promote culture but they also bureaucratize it, and, of course, live on it. It is hard for culture conditioned in such a way to be a place of resistance.

The strategy of simply "turning off" culture does not prove to be particularly effective either. The inhabitants of the little town of Farmington, Connecticut, described by Neil Postman in *Amusing Ourselves to Death,* decided to fight back against television. The local library organized a "Turn off Your TV" month and the inhabitants of Farmington followed suit. A certain Mrs. Babcock, preparing a new anti-TV campaign, issued the following statement: "Who knows whether our campaign will have the same significance this time as it had last year, when we had fantastic media coverage."

Those who are fully resigned say that we are participating in the funeral of a long and rich epoch in which there existed a phenomenon called art. "Art doesn't die because there isn't any more, it dies because there is too much," says Jean Baudrillard.

Those who feel that something is wrong with the concept of art, but think that things are reparable, have a formidable task in front of them. Within the complex and ambiguous structure of globalization, the "optimists" must first of all ask once again what art is, then set up a new system of aesthetic valuation and reevaluation. They have to open up space for market decontamination, for the mapping of the global "aesthetic" world, for the articulation of a new culture which could be called transnational. They could also reject everything and turn to a retro-utopia, which—if we accept Khlebnikov's eighty-year-old division of the participants in culture into creators and consumers—might restore a roof over the heads of the former: "romantics," "lunatics," "undesirables." Because a roof over their heads is what they have lost.

Noise

The realization of these and similar projects is possible within a culture of intellectual resistance. However, we live in a cultural environment that tends towards being conflict-free, in which the culture of monologue (or narcissism) has driven the culture of dialogue into the margins. The culture of monologue has taken a firm hold in all social spheres, including the intellectual sphere. The globalistic delirium of communication, which in itself implies dialogue, is realized in practice as monologue. In short, everyone rushes to broadcast his or her message to the world and self-promotion has become the social convention. An "artistic" or intellectual act is most often just a form of self-promotion. In the global market we are all sellers, even when it does not seem that way. Everyone automatically holds out his business card, everyone strives to be heard even when he has nothing to say. The texts of culture seem no longer to communicate with other texts of culture, neither traditional nor contemporary ones. They no longer establish interconnections, they do not confront one another, they do not support one another; each text circulates by itself, even when it is as like another text as two peas in a pod.

The messages of divine representatives—the Dalai Lama's gardening mantra about the blooming of a thousand flowers, or Madonna's translation ("Express yourself, don't suppress yourself")—have been adopted by the liberated masses with righteous dogmatism. In the globalized world, individuals feel their insignificance more than ever before. That is why everyone loudly trumpets his own sound and no one listens to anyone else. Listening is, they say, submission to the dominance of another. Speech is the realization of personal freedom and, therefore, dominance over those who agree to be dominated.

The global noise is indescribable. Even angels, whose job description includes patience and compassion, walk around with cotton balls in their ears. The only acceptable aesthetic choice that remains for people of good taste is silence.

Noise is music

That, of course, is just one way of looking at things. At the Forum 2000 conference held in Prague on the theme of globalization, the musician Peter Gabriel spoke about the beginnings of what is today the widespread trend of "world music." He happened to be in some African village, where instead of language as a means of communication they used noise: "We drummed together. We had fun making noise together," said Gabriel.

Many people define global culture as fundamentally postnational, diasporic, and hybrid. Some maintain that global culture has no center, but most believe that for now America is the most powerful producer and mediator of global culture. Europe, that "dazzling museum of a magnificent past," has proved incapable of "generating its own forms of mass cultural production," maintains Frederic Jameson in *The Cultures of Globalization*. "The death of modernism meant also the end of hegemonic European art and culture." Jameson believes that the attempt to establish "a new European cultural synthesis" did not offer sufficiently strong opposition to American domination. It is the same with the former socialist countries, which proved "incapable of generating an original culture." Only "mummified" culture, packaged with religious fundamentalism, successfully resists Americanization. Jameson further holds that technological power and money (Japan, for example) are still no guarantee of a sufficiently competitive cultural alternative to American cultural domination.

If all this is the case, if it is not a matter of money and technological power, then what is it that makes American culture so attractive to the rest of the world? "The United States is eminently suited to be a sort of cultural laboratory, a free-trade zone for generation, circulation, importation, and testing of materials for a world organized around diasporic diversity," writes Arjun Appadurai in his book *Modernity at Large*. "In some sense, this experiment is already under way. The United States is already a huge, fascinating garage sale for the rest of the world. It provides golf vacations and real estate for the Japanese; business-management ideologies and techniques for Europe and India; soap-opera ideas for Brazil and the Middle East; prime ministers for Yugoslavia; supply-side economics for Poland, Russia, and whoever else will try; Christian fundamentalism for Korea; and postmodern architecture for Hong Kong."

In America, global culture has found its most compatible ideological home. America has become a metaphor for a global, postnational, diasporic, and hybrid cultural mixture, for the culture of money and glamour, but also of new ideas; a metaphor for vitality, speed, the technological future; all in all a metaphor for modernity. America is the cultural ideal, but also the anti-ideal, an object of admiration but also of questioning. It is the dynamic generator of cultural wars, trends, and styles. It is the desired lifestyle. The world is "Americanized" as America is "Koreanized," "Hispanicized," "Russianized," "Japanized," "Vietnamized," "Cubanized." In other words, we are all America, whether we want to be or not. And we produce a global noise.

And while we are on the subject of noise, I'm not so sure after all about those angels with the cotton balls in their ears. Maybe they're not cotton balls but headphones.

2000

The Writer and His Future

A writer who decides to write about the future takes the conscious risk of one day appearing ludicrous, more ludicrous than usual. Making prophecies is a thankless task. Even if the predictions turn out to be accurate, their author's satisfaction is minimal because by that time the author is dead, or forever buried in the field of the trivial. Most often both. In the generally accepted scale of values, the present occupies first place, the past is second, and the future is last and most trivial. So any serious person hesitates to read the future.

Above all, the concept of the future has been discredited by utopias which, like every prophecy, have been realized in inverted form. Dictators, criminals, and other leaders have committed the greatest crimes precisely in its name, in the name of the future.

Today, among the ruins of utopian systems (above all communism) and wars (they say there are about a hundred being waged right now), the future seems to have disappeared somewhere. Especially the "bright future," the one that is now resting peacefully in the lexicon of communist ideas.

The future is no longer among us. I belong to a generation which sincerely believed it would fly to the moon. The first moon landing was a future shock of the first order, a global shot of adrenalin. The eyes of millions of people were suddenly turned towards the stars, and flight in that direction was, it seemed, just days away. Like tarot cards, the first moon flight had its inversion: along with the utopian idea of life on other planets came its ironic double. In America there is a funeral agency which guarantees that, after death, the urn with the client's ashes will be sent into space and his ashes scattered among the stars. Futuristic projections—moon flights, life on other planets, hibernation and waking in some future century—all end in poetic resignation, as ash among the stars.

I believed that one day I would buy a ticket for a flight to the moon. And not only that, my whole socialist childhood was filled with belief in a bright future. One in which white, yellow, and black people would be brothers and sisters. In which no one would be barefoot or hungry. In which there would be no oppression. In which everyone would produce according to his abilities and take according to his needs. In which there would be no frontiers. In which people would be happy.

I belong to a generation that experienced many firsts. I remember the first orange I saw and blissfully ate. The first fridge. The first TV set. Those first things merely fed our belief in the imminent bright future.

The future is the past which has not yet happened, someone once said. But my future has happened and is still happening. White, yellow, and black people have not become brothers and sisters. People are just as hungry, indeed they will be even hungrier, say the futurologists. In my country, the one that swore that there would be no more wars, there was war. The frontiers are still strong, indeed some are stronger than ever. Some walls fell but new ones have been built. Mankind gives no indication of living more happily. Technological progress has made the future visible: forests are disappearing before our eyes, deserts quietly spreading. And there are words to describe these phenomena: deforestation, desertification.

Out of the great utopian systems and global ideas, the future has continued to live where it always has. First, in subcultures, in sci-fi TV shows and movies, in cartoons and books. Whether it is brighter there, I don't know, I'm not a connoisseur. But it seems that apart from the fairy tale of the global handyman, Superman, the field of the trivial has not yet offered us much solace. The future has continued to live in highly specialized fields reserved for experts. Doctors focused on the future maintain that we are living in a posthuman age and are faced with imminent modification. Among other things it will soon be possible to build chips into the human brain to expand our mental capacities. On the other hand, futurologists predict that the basic method of transportation in the future will be not the personal flying machines so many of us hoped for, but bicycles. How our posthuman man with his expanded mental capacities will manage on a bicycle is something that we leave to the futurologists.

What has changed in the last fifty years or so for the ordinary person? He lives longer, at least so we are told, but then again he dies more frequently. He lives more quickly and communicates with unimaginable speed. From the world of already miraculous fax machines, it took just a year or two to find ourselves in cyberspace. Is cyberspace the great delirious utopia we are already living in, without our having managed to notice it?

The price of conquering distance and speed is that we are left with a very stunted sense of time. The centuries behind us remain obscure. People cannot even cope with the history of their own life. They have calendars and Rolex watches but hardly remember what they had for lunch yesterday. Maybe it is because of this inability to cope with time that the human imagination of the future has remained in the realm of the trivial: the future is a fairy tale for adults. Maybe, when God made people, He screwed up and forgot to build into our brains an important chip, the one for understanding time, leaving only an empty, indifferent space where that chip should be. So we are left with reproduction. This is the way to understand time: when I am no longer here, my children will be. Or my clones.

Let us play a game of literary palm-reading and consult the tarot cards. Let us take a look at what will become of literature. It can't hurt, and literature is, after all, our field.

The tarot cards say that there will no longer be any literature in the future. Or at least not as we know it. If we are on the threshold of a posthuman age, as the scientists maintain, then surely human activities, including literature, should become posthuman. Besides, literature has already been greatly modified: we can find it on CD, on the Internet, in interactive computer games, in hypertext. "If *literature* has died, *literary activity* continues with unabated, if not increased vigor," writes Alvin Kernan in the controversial book *The Death of Literature*. Traditional writers will disappear, like umbrella menders. "Real literature" will be a rarity, because no one will know what "real literature" is, any more than they know how to recognize the symptoms of bubonic plague, or what a bedbug is.

Is it all really like this? Literary life today seems to imply the opposite. More books are being produced than ever, they never looked better, bookstores were never more attractive, writers never had such opportunities to become global stars as they do today. So why am I grumbling when there is no reason to?

When Robert Mitchum was asked what he thought about himself as a film star, he replied: "Nothing. Especially when I think that Rin Tin Tin is also a star." If I were to ask a writer today what he thought about himself as a writer, he might reply: "Nothing. Especially when I think that if Rin Tin Tin were alive today, his memoirs would be a best-seller."

Like many other human activities, literature has lost the exclusiveness it once had. This happened imperceptibly, and the reasons for it are many. The institutions of national literatures, for example, which set up a whole network of protective forms—university departments, academies, schools, literary studies, institutes, archives—have gradually dried up or lost their significance. Writers, some sooner, some later, greeted the disappearance of all institutional constraints (political, national, religious, ideological, literary-traditional) with satisfaction. Before them opened up the broad field of the ideologically indifferent literary market and, full of enthusiasm and belief in equal literary competition (may the best writer win!), they accepted the market. They did, of course, foresee that in the absence of ideologies, the market itself could become an ideology. "The world of business, it seems, is becoming the world, period. The market is politics, the office is society, the brand is equivalent to human identity," writes Erik Barnouw in *Conglomerates and the Media*.

Having lost its exclusivity, literature has paradoxically gained in exclusivity. Not everyone can be a surgeon, a mathematician, or a pianist, but it turns out that anyone can publish a book, and that's why many have crowded into the literary marketplace. Literature has thus become a passport to eternity accessible to everyone, a ticket to a journey in the orbit of the chosen. Suddenly it turns out that we are living in an age when everyone has the right to a voice but no one listens.

Thirty years ago, everyone ran the market race in his own category: juniors with juniors, seniors with seniors. Today the exhausting market marathon is run by everyone at the same time. Thirty years ago, the boundary between "high" and "low" literature still existed, and everyone was satisfied. High literature had its admirers, trivial literature did too. The polite old lady, high literature, was the first to offer her hand to trivial literature. Fascinated by the popularity of trivial literature but sure of her own high position on the scale of literary values, high literature began to play with trivial literature, as it had before as well. It adopted its strategies, parodied it, and self-confidently paraded its own art. High literature at the time was still protected by a strong theory of literature, the blossoming of literary-interpretative schools, diligent literary departments at universities, ambitious critics, lengthy studies in thick magazines, arbiters of good taste, serious and respected editors and independent publishers. Today those thick literary magazines are disappearing, serious editors lose their jobs too often to remain serious, literature is no longer a prestigious field of study, and books are divided into those which "work" and those which "don't work," for books are simply a commodity of the publishing industry. Criticism and the theory and history of literature have mutated into cultural studies, and it is easy to imagine that university departments will soon start to offer courses in literary marketing along with courses in literary history—there are already courses in cultural management. The concept of *literature* is disappearing, and its place is increasingly being taken by *books*.

Not only have the dividing lines faded between high and trivial literature, but many people no longer know the meaning of these old-fashioned terms. A writer who aspires to the category of so-called "serious" literature has lost his social sphere; he finds it hard to distinguish the face of his addressee; it seems to him that people do not understand him and he tries to adapt his language in order to be understood. What's more, many serious writers are convinced that their ability to penetrate the market is a measure of their quality. Readers are equally convinced. And publishers zealously nourish that conviction.

In the meantime, trivial literature has also mutated and gradually laid claim to the exclusive realm of high literature. Just as high literature played with the strategies of trivial literature, trivial literature decorates itself with the honors of high literature and steals its language. Mass culture never misses a chance to make high-literature references. Trivial literature has infiltrated the ivy-covered walls of academia, into university curricula, and it has blown the arbiters of good taste into elitist anonymity, destroyed the independent publishers, replaced unattractive magazines and serious studies with attractive blurbs and newspaper advertisements, lured gurus and promoters over to its side. Along the way, the products of mass culture have mutated and become "mid-cult," which "behaves as though it respects the standards of High Culture while in fact it waters them down and vulgarizes them" (Richard Senett). Which was not so hard to do. There are fewer and fewer of those who know how to distinguish the authentic from the false. If they do know, they do not have the will to fight a losing battle. If they do have the will, they are unlikely to get media space for evaluation, because media space is reserved for books which "work" or at least "should work." Besides, the very distinction between "authentic" and "false" has been intellectually uninteresting for a long time. As is the old-fashioned terminology of aesthetic value. Because what are aesthetic values after all? It's a matter of who, or what, determines them. "Money creates taste," suggests one slogan, convincingly.

Identity politics has also contributed to the way the Western canon, the traditional system of literary-aesthetic values, has collapsed like a house of cards. Equality between a multitude of different literary expressions has replaced the monopoly. Women's literature, for example, has realized its full dignity, created women's studies, women's reading of literary history, a female interpretation of traditional literary texts, has begun to reassess literature and asserted the right to a different literary taste, reevaluated trivial literature whose authors were women, and created in the market a strong female reading public, its consumers. African-American literature, too, has created its own institutions, studies, criticism, and audience and enriched the literary market. Today it would be impossible to say what Saul Bellow once said—"When the Zulu have a Tolstoy, then perhaps I shall read them"—without being rightly accused of cultural chauvinism.

In the increasingly global literary marketplace there is everything, for every taste: Mongolian literature and the literature of Trinidad, emigré literature and the literatures of various ethnic groups, the literatures of different sexual orientations and subgroups: Bosnian-gay and Jewish-lesbian. The once cold interpretative schools which desensualized a literary text have been replaced by the warm relativity of Otherness. Anything goes, and everyone has his audience.

But still, does all this mean that individual expression (which, incidentally, ought to be the presupposition of any artistic literary text) is now in the ascendant? Does it mean that literature itself has been enriched with a multitude of individual statements? Has individual speech become more individual? Have literary techniques become more varied and fertile, and are the perceptions offered by literary texts really unique?

The opposite has happened, or at least so it seems. The individual voice is increasingly rare. Every voice, every text, is slotted into the market niche of the moment, the buzzword of the moment, the codes of the market. In order to be heard and understood, the writer consciously or unconsciously adapts his voice to the demands of the market, to his potential readers at that moment. Even if it never occurs to him, even if he refuses, this translation into the language of the market happens without his control: in the market itself, in reception, in reading. Thus the established right to the authenticity of Otherness rebounds on the writer and his text like a boomerang.

Escaping from one trap, the writer has flown into another. The writer today is more than ever before plastered with identity labels, and these labels determine his place in the literary market and the kind of understanding there can be between himself and his readers. "Identities" do, admittedly, facilitate market communication, but they badly reduce the meaning of the text, impoverishing it or simply distorting it. The literary text is read more than ever with a key: gender, racial, national, ethnic, cultural, sexual, political. It is also diminished by a market which sells books just like any other commodity, according to categories and not according to value. Milan Kundera's *The Joke* can be found in the humor section and György Konrád's *A Feast in the Garden* among the gardening books.

The contemporary writer who aspires to the category of so-called high literature is confused by the absence of a value system, and the reader finds it even harder to cope with this absence. But the space out of which the traditionalist promoters of value have been driven—professors of literature, literary critics, intellectuals—has not, of course, been left empty. It has been occupied by powerful and attractive arbiters, from Oprah Winfrey to Amazon.com. It has been occupied by salesmen: an editor's greatest praise is that the "marketing people" are pleased with a manuscript; these mythical "marketing people," when mentioned by the editor (and increasingly by writers themselves), sound like the Nobel Prize committee. Finally, unlike the perpetually hesitant intellectuals, the market itself does not shrink from value judgments. On the contrary, advertising messages are judgmental and imperative. *This is beautiful!* goes one advertising slogan.

As a rule, the market is never subversive, it does not destroy the aesthetic canon but integrates it and exploits it for its own purposes. Books, blurbs, and literary reviews (which increasingly resemble extended blurbs) abound with references to canonical figures: "this book is an explosive mix of Beckett and Dumas," "worthy of Kafka," "Proust would be envious." But a trick of parallelism uses these canonical values in the interests of market relativism. A recent ad, which shows computer-generated figures of da Vinci, Rembrandt, and Toulouse-Lautrec getting happily behind the wheels of their new Mercedes, makes a witty connection between values: what Leonardo da Vinci is to art, the Mercedes is to cars. Less wittily, a successful writer of pornographic novels produced her own self-promotional blurb in a TV interview: "There's no difference. Umberto Eco is best in his branch of literature, I'm best in mine."

The so-called serious writer lives a kind of underground life. He conceals his high literary aspirations and his literary taste for fear that he will be accused of elitism. And it really happens, the numerically superior promoters of mass culture, the cyber-ecstatics, culture-optimists, and anti-elitists, readily pounce on every "literary bore" of the kind who keeps a photograph of Nabokov on his desk. Admittedly, out of good taste, the "bore" has removed Nabokov's photograph because even Nabokov has been co-opted into a marketing label (for books which are packaged as "anti-trash," real, elite literature). The crafty market turns every criticism of it to its own profit. It is the market, then, and not conservatives, elitists, and culture-pessimists which sets trends and creates literary taste. If one day the market decides to make a global best-seller of *A Man without Qualities,* that is what Musil's novel will become.

At a time when books are written, published, and read more than ever before, the writer and the reader are the loneliest and most threatened species. Salman Rushdie writes: "Readers, finding themselves unable to track their way through the rain forest of junk fiction and made cynical by the debased language of hyperbole with which every book is garlanded, give up. They buy a couple of prizewinners a year, perhaps one or two books by writers whose names they recognize, and flee. Overpublishing and overhyping put people off reading. It is not just a question of too many novels chasing too few readers but a question of too many novels actually chasing readers away."

It sometimes seems as though we were living in the upside-down anti-utopia of Ray Bradbury's *Fahrenheit 451.* Bradbury's novel describes a repressive society of happiness sedated with pills and the television screen, a society in which books are prohibited, a society of book burners. But we are living in the world of a gleaming shopping mall, where books are advertised in the attractive language of Coca-Cola ads, while we can access information about books, and buy them, simply by pressing a button on our computer keyboards.

So, what is left for the writer "after the end of art"?

    a) He can set out in the opposite direction and defend criteria of high literary value. For "literature is not a school. Literature must assume an audience that is more cultivated than the writer himself. Whether such an audience exists or not is not important. The writer addresses a reader who knows more about it than he does himself; he invents himself as someone who knows more than he really does, in order to be able to address someone who knows even more. Literature has no other choice than to erect obstacles and maintain the pretence, following the logic of a situation which can only get worse." So writes Italo Calvino in his essay "For Whom Do We Write, or A Hypothetical Bookshelf."

b) He can abandon himself to the cultural orgy of the moment, join the rich network of transnational culture, participate in the acceleration of transcultural, posthistorical, postcolonial, postnational, poststate, postart, posthuman, postliterary, and postmodern modernity.

c) He can reconcile himself to the fact that some species die out not because of a hostile environment but because of the structure of their own organisms. Pandas are dying out because, among other things, their lengthy chewing of bamboo shoots does not give them time for procreation. The writer is like a panda: the world around him is too fast and complex and his language is too slow. Apart from that, the writer's addressee, the reader, is no longer a person who sits in an armchair deeply absorbed in reading a book. The reader is a person constantly on the move: he reads in the plane, or at the gym with headphones on, or listens to books on tape while driving.

Writers can also turn their long-since-reported death into a worthy artistic gesture and accept the services of the funeral agency mentioned at the beginning of this essay. They can start paying their funeral dues now, and soulfully imagine their ashes scattered among the stars. Not even I, whose profession is invention, would be able to imagine a more poetic happy ending.

2000

7 ——————————— Closing

They're funny things, Accidents. You never have them till you're having them.

The Seventh Screw

Anyone who has been through the experience known as *completely renovating one's apartment* knows that everything is in the hands of the workmen. Workmen are our natural enemies. They exist in this world only to make our lives difficult, throw us into debt, force us down on our knees, prove that we are nobodies, that our home is not our castle, that everything we know is worthless. There is a Slavic saying—*Mind rules, body shifts rock*—which means that everyone is supposed to do their own job. But it's not true. Whoever shifts rock rules.

The first workman to enter my apartment was Frank, a Dutchman. In just two days Frank pulled down everything that had to be pulled down, destroyed everything that had to be destroyed, and took away all the garbage that had to be taken away. Today I think that Frank was my guardian angel, who disguised his identity by agreeing to do an enormous job for a little pocket money. Frank was a sworn enemy of all kinds of constraints: state, marital, family, bureaucratic, residential. He did not have a credit card, a bank account, a telephone number, a tax number, an address—why would an angel need such nonsense! If, by some miracle, he should ever happen to read these lines, he will be doing so in the Himalayas, the Andes, Tibet, or some such place. Frank confided in me that he only felt like *a man* at great altitudes.

After Frank came Ben with his entourage, Paula and Honza.

Honza was a Czech, a peace-loving giant almost seven feet tall, who came to Amsterdam from time to time to earn a few guilders illegally.

"Hrabal, Hašek, or Čapek?" I said foolishly, holding out my hand to Honza.

"Hašek!" he responded instantly.

Paula was a strong lady with a soft moustache on her upper lip. In her younger days she had been a truck driver and a lover of heavy motorcycles. She had ridden from New York to Los Angeles several times with American bikers.

Ben himself was an electrician, a master of his craft. Apart from the love of his craft, Ben nurtured a weakness for unusual people. These unusual people were as a rule far larger and stronger than he was. I found this out later, when I met Ben's girlfriend.

I no longer remember who sent Roy. He appeared at the same time as Niki and Davor, my countrymen. Niki was a passionate film buff. Being with Roy, an American of Italian origin from Brooklyn, was almost as exciting for Niki as painting walls with Robert De Niro. Roy also enchanted Niki with his love of sailboats. He always had a catalogue with him listing the types and prices of sailboats. Davor had never been to America either. Roy easily fired both their imaginations. Roy was a carpenter, and Niki and Davor were guys who could do everything, from painting walls to fixing tiles.

I was suspicious of Roy from the start. He wanted twice as much an hour as I paid Niki and Davor. He was a trickster, quick to take money, an altogether shady person. However, workmen were hard to come by. And Niki and Davor both took Roy's side.

In the evening, over an improvised meal and a bottle or two of wine, some details of Roy's life began to float to the surface in nightmarish disorder.

He had been living in Amsterdam for a year now. He had stayed because of a Dutch girl. He had a construction company in America. He had made a million dollars several times over and then lost it, made it and lost it again. It's easy to make a million in America, but it's hard to hang onto it, he said. He had heaps of money, he was a "king." He used to renovate the apartments of rich Americans, he had seen everything.

He had a wife and son. He often called his son. But he stayed in close contact only with his sister. His sister had her own family, two children and a husband, a hardened alcoholic. His sister was a master of survival.

Their mother had been a real beauty. She used to be a fashion model. She had Roy and his sister when she was very young. People would often think that his own mother was his girlfriend, she still looked so young. Their father was a tyrant, a pig, that's what. Their mother left him and married Steve. Uncle Steve was rich. He was no longer among the living. His mother was in a wheelchair now. Whenever he's there, Roy takes care of her.

Roy takes care of all of them, they are all on his back. Including his ex-wife, a real bitch. He had found her in bed with one of his own workers, a black guy. They tried to kill him, they wanted him out of the way so they could take over the business. He barely pulled through. The bullet missed his spine by a fraction of an inch. That's how he got his grey hair.

It wasn't bad in Europe, but he'd never stay. The Dutch girl was still a kid, she didn't know what to do with her life. And he knew she only liked him in bed.

He had relatives in Italy, in the Mafia, of course, they were all in the Mafia. He didn't know Italian, but he still felt Italian. But he preferred France, he had spent time there as well.

His sister remained his only support. They had plans together, he and his sister. Big plans. They were all going to move to Montana, they'd build a house there and live together. They would breed horses, his sister had it all planned already. In any case there was going to be a great flood in a few years' time. America would disappear from the face of the earth, his sister had asked around and heard it from people in the know. Montana would be the only place left.

His life was more exciting than a novel. If there were anyone to write it down, it would be a real best-seller. Who knows, maybe he'd pick up a pen himself one day. In Montana, on the ranch, when he got older. He got a prize for an essay at school once.

Before long, Roy started to get on my nerves. I was irritated by his arrogance, as though he were some kind of prince doing forced labor, and by his frequent bad temper, his changing moods, the fact that he turned us all, with unbelievable speed, into the hostages of his stormy emotions. As though we didn't have any emotions of our own.

Once I came across him with a guitar in his hands. He was entertaining Niki and Davor by singing a song which he had supposedly composed in my honor. I paid dearly for Roy's "performance." By the hour. Roy spent more and more hours shirking and it turned out that he wasn't able to finish any of the jobs he began. He would put three tiles down in the hall, and then start painting the kitchen. He would paint half a wall and start something else. He began coming later and later and leaving earlier and earlier. He wanted me to pay him every day, sometimes even in advance. If I tried to say anything, he would take offence. He took offence over every trifle.

Several times he launched into long, uncontrolled, bitter monologues in front of us: everyone exploited him, everyone was on his back, they were all fucking bitches, his sister, his mother, his ex-wife, why didn't they all leave him alone, he was "king" of his craft, he had built dozens of houses from cellar to roof, laid miles of tiles and pipes, painted so many walls with his own hands that if someone put them all together it would turn out he had painted a whole fucking Iowa. He could pack up all his stuff this minute and go. There was work like this everywhere, like shit on the road.

We listened to him, pinned to the spot. I didn't know what to do. I was even a little afraid of him.

"Roy makes me feel like I have a land mine in the apartment," I said to Niki and Davor.

But Davor assured me that Roy was a good workman and I had to keep him on. Roy keeps up a good tempo, he said.

One morning Roy appeared and told us he had spent the night writing the introduction to his future novel, *The Seven Screws.*

"Should I read it to you?" he asked, taking two pages out of his pocket.

"Why not," said Niki and Davor, looking in my direction.

At that moment I was kneeling, getting my hands filthy. I was grouting the floor tiles, which Roy had omitted to do the previous day. I was overcome by an indescribable rage. "*Seven Screws*"?! What next!

I was a freelance writer, I could barely make ends meet, and the expense of renovation had landed me with debts that I could not see how I would ever repay. What am I doing, I wondered? Have I gone stark, raving mad? I've been exhausting myself for days with physical labor, for days I haven't been able to write a single line, I'm spending a fortune on a jerk whose last name I don't even know, for what? So that this jerk can write a novel about his life? What kind of a nightmare is this?

I stood up and, gasping for breath, I hissed:

"You're fired, Roy!"

I must have looked terrible, because Roy left without a word, his tail between his legs. Niki, Davor and I completed the work. We all felt relieved after Roy's departure. Even Davor, who had shown the most understanding for Roy. He mentioned to me that Roy was going to give up his apartment in a day or two and move in with him.

The work was entering its final phase. The only thing left was to lay the wooden floor. The boards had been bought. But Davor and Niki didn't know how to do it. I searched for workmen, I called up friends asking whether they knew of anyone. No one was available. The first one I could get wouldn't be able to come for three months. I was in despair.

Cautiously, Davor suggested that we ask Roy. He was going to be leaving for France in a few days anyway and then going back home, to America. I agreed; I didn't have any choice. I gave the three of them two days to finish the job.

When I came back on the third day, the floor was done. Roy was glowing with satisfaction. Niki and Davor looked triumphant. I could breathe.

Roy asked me whether he could give his sister my e-mail address. Of course, I said.

"When she writes, tell her I was good. Tell her what a fantastic floor I laid," he said in a pleading tone. Suddenly I felt sorry for him. He looked like a big child.

The next morning, even though there was nothing to do, Roy appeared in the apartment as usual, in his working clothes, jeans and a t-shirt covered in paint. He was also wearing an Armani jacket of a rather old-fashioned cut.

"I used to have dozens of these," he said, pointing at the jacket. "Just a few years ago, I could have any chick in the world! The chicks used to scratch at my door to get in!"

For the first time I noticed that Roy was a good-looking man. Kind of like Elvis. Medium height, well-built, green eyes framed in thick black lashes like a doll's, abundant black hair well-sprinkled with grey.

He hung around for a while, looking through the empty apartment, checking whether the floor screws were properly tightened.

"Good, isn't it?" he asked, looking at the floor.

"Yes," I said.

"I could use the leftover wood to make bookshelves. . . ."

This was true, there was a lot of wood left over, and I hadn't known what to do with it.

All day I watched Roy making bookshelves. In the empty apartment with its freshly painted walls, with the shiny, light-wood floor, bathed in sunlight from the windows, Roy looked magnificent. He worked without a moment's rest, completely absorbed. Under Roy's able hands, the remaining wood turned into an elegant bookcase.

"That's a gift from me! In honor of the house!" he said, thumping his chest.

Roy left for Paris. He borrowed some two thousand guilders from Davor. As soon as he reached America, he was going to send for Davor to join him. America is a country where you can make money. He, Roy, has his boys, the workmen, who follow in the wake of hurricanes. Wherever a hurricane strikes, they immediately pick up their tools and rush off there.

As I was cleaning the apartment, I found several of Roy's cassettes (Bruce Springsteen), a paperback thriller, and some worn-out sneakers in the cupboard with the electricity meter. I threw everything out. Two messages arrived at my e-mail address from Roy's sister, a real-estate puff piece about the price of land and houses in Montana and information about a network of American producers of handmade teddy bears. I remembered Roy had said that his sister had skilled hands and made teddy bears. I didn't reply. What could I have answered?

Niki, Davor, and I stayed in contact. They often came to see me. Roy was a frequent topic of our conversation. Davor told us more details that he had heard from Roy.

Roy was obsessed by his Uncle Steve, Davor told us. This "uncle" was a powerful mafioso, connected with everyone, the CIA, the FBI, who knows what else. He smuggled cocaine, tons of cocaine. He had fabricated his own death. Even Roy's mother didn't know about it. Uncle Steve was living in Mexico, under another name of course, and Roy was the only person who knew where he was. Uncle Steve often took Roy along with him. Uncle Steve had introduced Roy to the life of the Mafia. Once, Roy had watched them cutting the big toes off of some poor wretch, tying his hands and hanging him up and leaving him to bleed slowly.

Roy heard a lot about the New York docks. Before the fish was sent to the New York markets, it was cleaned on the fishing boats. And then the boats would go back to the open sea and pump the fish innards down into the sea. At least that's what Davor understood from Roy's stories. Sometimes, along with the fish innards, they sent the occasional corpse riddled with bullets down to the depths as well. The fishermen and the Mafia had struck an "ecological" deal. Roy saw it all. That's why he was dangerous, because he knew too much. And that was why he was afraid of going back to America. He was wanted by the IRS. He owed tens of thousands of dollars. It wasn't much, he'd pay it off once he was back on his feet. If his sister sent him the passport of a relative who looked just like him, he'd be able to get back without any trouble.

Davor told us all this. His English may not have been all that good, but it sounded convincing. As I said, Roy was a shady type from the outset.

Roy never got in touch, about the two thousand guilders or anything else. Davor tried to call Roy's sister once. Her number was the only thing Roy had left him. The sister hung up on him.

A year had passed since Roy's disappearance.

In the bathroom, Roy had made a false beam of waterproofed wood, a kind of mask to hide the ugly pipes and main tap for the water supply, which was placed quite high up, out of reach. It occurred to me that I had not checked where exactly that tap was, and I climbed onto a ladder. I reached out with my hand and, tucked behind the tap, found a sheaf of papers.

They were the first two pages—a page and a half—of Roy's novel, *The Seven Screws.* Roy must have put the pages there when he, Davor, and Niki were laying the floor. As though on the one hand he wanted me to find them, but at the same time he didn't. No one would ever look in the place he had hidden them, except when there was a problem of some kind and it was necessary to turn off the water.

I sat down and read Roy's pages carefully.

Roy began the first page with the observation that he was *rapidly approaching middle age,* and that he wanted with his confession to leave a *testament* and put right *the injustice he had done himself, and which others had done him.* Perhaps by writing this work, he would succeed in *driving out the demons that tormented him through long days and sleepless nights.* For he, Roy, was no longer sure who he was, was he a *shadow,* or the *ghost of who he once was?* He begged the reader to *try to understand what he was about to disclose on the pages which followed,* even though he knew it was full of *bitterness and self-pity.* That was why he was not thinking of asking for *forgiveness for himself,* but for *that boy who had so longed to be loved and accepted.*

The story which was to follow would be the story of that boy, of seven Brooklyn boys who had tried to find a way out of their lives and had *taken what could not be given to them,* of seven boys who had made a pact so firm that it could be broken only by *death.*

Why was the novel called *The Seven Screws?*

Small titanium screws removed from one of the boy's legs after a bone operation. Seven screws for seven boys who would become seven violent men who knew no fear. Seven screws for seven destinies. . . .

Roy's short introduction was full of these repetitions, as though he were repeating a mantra which had long ago settled in his head, and he could not get out of that verbal trap. But still, as I read the last sentences, I shuddered.

I'm writing this story as a testimony to these young men capable of unspeakable atrocities, as you will soon see. And, in writing this story, I'll set my soul free so that it may find peace. Because I'm not just a man. I'm the seventh screw.

That was all.

In the end, there remains the question of what exactly all these trifles—from the renovation of the apartment to neurotic carpenters—have to do with books and literature. What connection does Roy have with the content of this book?

The mere detail that he made bookshelves for me with his own hands assures Roy a place in these pages.

But there's more. Hiding his manuscript in a place where he knew that I wouldn't soon find it, Roy left behind a message in a bottle. Roy's muddled text was typed on an electric typewriter, and I very much doubt that there is a copy. If something happens to Roy, if he disappears from his own life as he disappeared from mine, these words in my book will be some kind of proof of Roy's existence and his desire to leave a testimony about the events that had made him "a shadow of what he once was." They are a concession on my part, "for free"; symbolic compensation for the bookshelf.

Roy's story can also be read as a fable about the fact that the divide between the "recognized" and the "unrecognized" is fragile. Either can change places with the other at any moment. Had I not, after all, been doing Roy's work, while Roy took my place for a moment? Kneeling, my hands covered in tiling grout, I had been carrying out some kind of symbolic penance for an excess of writer's self-confidence.

The beginning of Roy's novel was in fact a perfect example of how to write a book proposal. It was rich with references—the number seven; the seven Brooklyn samurai; the romantic topoi of ghosts, shadows, and demons; the traditional rhetoric of opening a novel by calling on the reader to "forgive" the author's "sins"—and that is why it was so effective. There is no more effective hook for catching the reader's attention than the request that he participate in discovering a secret. Hadn't we, Niki, Davor and I, been caught on that hook too? Roy had remained a secret for us.

Roy's story is in fact the story of how stories come into being. *The fox is the god of cunning and treachery. The fox is the god of writers,* writes Boris Pilnyak. If he ever does write his confession, Roy will have to steal the stories of people who may or may not have existed, which is, after all, what every writer does. Writing this story about Roy, I slunk up like a fox and snatched part of it from him. Maybe those two pages left behind were not a message in a bottle, but bait.

Among the reasons Roy lists as driving him to write his book, he mentions "doing justice." The belief in doing justice—aesthetic, literary, political, intimate, whatever kind—is one of the most powerful triggers that moves the hand to pick up the pen, no matter what the artistic results are. I myself seem to be pursuing some kind of "justice" too.

Books will exist as long as there are stories which are convinced that they *must* be written and as long as there are readers (writers are readers too!) who as they read those stories are convinced that they *have* to be rewritten. And as far as literary art itself is concerned, who knows, perhaps the whole trick begins the moment that someone who is a carpenter by profession writes the sentence *I'm not just a man. I'm the seventh screw*—and it does not make you laugh.

As I said, we have not heard anything from Roy for a whole year. He left behind him a bookcase and a page and a half of his future novel. Perhaps he is still in Paris, living as a bum. Perhaps some Paris lady has taken him on as her escort, and Roy is walking around Paris in new Armani jackets, back in the best days of his life. Perhaps he has joined the Italian Mafia and is participating in *unspeakable atrocities.* Perhaps he stowed away on the wrong boat and sailed to Havana. Perhaps, as I write these lines, he is sitting in a workshop in Havana learning how to roll cigars. Perhaps he has already left Cuba. Perhaps he managed to reach Miami in some dilapidated sailboat. Perhaps, as a Cuban refugee in his own country, he is working on the black market, repairing houses destroyed by the last mighty hurricane. Perhaps he is in Montana, in a house he has built with his own hands, from cellar to roof. There—in an attic room, at a desk facing the window, looking out from time to time at the green pastures where horses graze—Roy is writing his novel, *The Seven Screws.* Perhaps at the moment I am writing these lines, I am living a parallel life in Roy's pages, a life about which I know nothing.

2000

About the Author

In addition to her other essay collections (*Have a Nice Day* and *The Culture of Lies*) Dubravka Ugresic has written several fictional works, including *In the Jaws of Life and Other Stories, Fording the Stream of Consciousness,* and *The Museum of Unconditional Surrender.* The international prizes she has been awarded for her writing include the Swiss "Charles Veillon" European Essay Prize (for *The Culture of Lies*), the Dutch Versetsprijs, or Artist in Resistance Prize, the Austrian State Prize for European Literature, the German Sudwestfunk Prize, and the Heinrich Mann Prize. In 2003, she was also a finalist for the Strega Prize.

Born and raised in the former Yugoslavia, she left her homeland in 1993 for political reasons. Since that time she has taught at a variety of American universities including Wesleyan, University of North Carolina at Chapel Hill, UCLA, and Harvard. She currently lives in Amsterdam.

SELECTED DALKEY ARCHIVE PAPERBACKS

FOR A FULL LIST OF PUBLICATIONS, VISIT:
www.dalkeyarchive.com

SELECTED DALKEY ARCHIVE PAPERBACKS

FOR A FULL LIST OF PUBLICATIONS, VISIT:
www.dalkeyarchive.com